A TASTE OF HONEY

A Taste of Honey

A PLAY BY

SHELAGH DELANEY

Grove Press
New York

Printed in the United States of America

Library of Congress Catalog Card Number: 59-8206
ISBN 0-8021-3185-9

Grove Press
841 Broadway
New York, NY 10003

00 01 02 03   45 44 43 42 41 40 39 38 37

A TASTE OF HONEY

This play was first presented by Theatre Workshop at the Theatre Royal, Stratford, London E15, on 27 May 1958.

On 10 February 1959 the play was presented by Donald Albery and Oscar Lewenstein Ltd, at Wyndham's Theatre, London, with the following cast:

HELEN	Avis Bunnage
JOSEPHINE, *her daughter*	Frances Cuka
PETER, *her friend*	Nigel Davenport
THE BOY	Clifton Jones
GEOFFREY	Murray Melvin

THE APEX JAZZ TRIO	Johnny Wallbank (*cornet*)
	Barry Wright (*guitar*)
	Christopher Capon (*double bass*)
SETTING BY	John Bury
COSTUMES BY	Una Collins

The play is set in Salford, Lancashire, today

Directed by Joan Littlewood

Act One

SCENE ONE

The stage represents a comfortless flat in Manchester and the street outside. Jazz music. Enter HELEN, *a semi-whore, and her daughter,* JO. *They are loaded with baggage.*

HELEN: Well! This is the place.

JO: And I don't like it.

HELEN: When I find somewhere for us to live I have to consider something far more important than your feelings . . . the rent. It's all I can afford.

JO: You can afford something better than this old ruin.

HELEN: When you start earning you can start moaning.

JO: Can't be soon enough for me. I'm cold and my shoes let water . . . what a place . . . and we're supposed to be living off her immoral earnings.

HELEN: I'm careful. Anyway, what's wrong with this place? Everything in it's falling apart, it's true, and we've no heating – but there's a lovely view of the gasworks, we share a bathroom with the community and this wallpaper's contemporary. What more do you want? Anyway it'll do for us. Pass me a glass, Jo.

JO: Where are they?

HELEN: I don't know.

JO: You packed 'em. She'd lose her head if it was loose.

HELEN: Here they are. I put 'em in my bag for safety. Pass me that bottle – it's in the carrier.

JO: Why should I run round after you? [*Takes whisky bottle from bag.*]

HELEN: Children owe their parents these little attentions.

JO: I don't owe you a thing.

HELEN: Except respect, and I don't seem to get any of that.

JO: Drink, drink, drink, that's all you're fit for. You make me sick.

HELEN: Others may pray for their daily bread, I pray for . . .

JO: Is that the bedroom?

HELEN: It is. Your health, Jo.

JO: We're sharing a bed again, I see.

HELEN: Of course, you know I can't bear to be parted from you.

JO: What I wouldn't give for a room of my own! God! It's freezing! Isn't there any sort of fire anywhere, Helen?

HELEN: Yes, there's a gas-propelled thing somewhere.

JO: Where?

HELEN: Where? What were you given eyes for? Do you want me to carry you about? Don't stand there shivering; have some of this if you're so cold.

JO: You know I don't like it.

HELEN: Have you tried it?

JO: No.

HELEN: Then get it down you! [*She wanders around the room searching for fire.*] "Where!" she says. She can never see anything till she falls over it. Now, where's it got to? I know I saw it here somewhere . . . one of those shilling in the slot affairs; the landlady pointed it out to me as part of the furniture and fittings. I don't know. Oh! It'll turn up. What's up with you now?

JO: I don't like the smell of it.

HELEN: You don't smell it, you drink it! It consoles you.

JO: What do you need consoling about?

HELEN: Life! Come on, give it to me if you've done with it. I'll soon put it in a safe place. [*Drinks.*]

JO: You're knocking it back worse than ever.

HELEN: Oh! Well, it's one way of passing time while I'm

old
before John

waiting for something to turn up. And it usually does if I drink hard enough. Oh my God! I've caught a shocking cold from somebody. Have you got a clean hanky, Jo? Mine's wringing wet with dabbing at my nose all day.

JO: Have this, it's nearly clean. Isn't that light awful? I do hate to see an unshaded electric light bulb dangling from the ceiling like that.

HELEN: Well, don't look at it then.

JO: Can I have that chair, Helen? I'll put my scarf round it. [JO *takes chair from* HELEN, *stands on it and wraps her scarf round light bulb—burning herself in the process.*]

HELEN: Wouldn't she get on your nerves? Just when I was going to take the weight off my feet for five minutes. Oh! my poor old nose.

JO: Christ! It's hot.

HELEN: Why can't you leave things alone? Oh! she gets me down. I'll buy a proper shade tomorrow. It's running like a tap. This is the third hanky today.

JO: Tomorrow? What makes you think we're going to live that long? The roof's leaking!

HELEN: Is it? No, it's not, it's just condensation.

JO: Was it raining when you took the place?

HELEN: It is a bit of a mess, isn't it.

JO: You always have to rush off into things. You never think.

HELEN: Oh well, we can always find something else.

JO: But what are you looking for? Every place we find is the same.

HELEN: Oh! Every time I turn my head my eyeballs hurt. Can't we have a bit of peace for five minutes?

JO: I'll make some coffee.

HELEN: Do what you like. I feel rotten. I've no business being out of bed.

JO: Where's the kitchen?

HELEN: Where's the – through there. I have to be really bad before I can go to bed, though. It's the only redeeming feature in this entire lodging house. I've got it in my throat now too. I hope you're going to make full use of it.

JO: There's a gas stove in here.

HELEN: It hurts when I swallow. Of course there is!

JO: It looks a bit ancient. How do I light it?

HELEN: How do I – with a match. Wouldn't she drive you mad?

JO: I know that, but which knob do I turn?

HELEN: Turn 'em all, you're bound to find the right one in the end. She can't do a thing for herself, that girl. Mind you don't gas yourself. Every time I comb my hair it goes right through me. I think it's more than a cold, you know – more likely it's 'flu! Did you find it?

[*Loud bang.*]

JO: Yes.

HELEN: The way she bangs about! I tell you, my head's coming off.

JO: Won't be long now. Who lives here besides us, Helen? Any young people?

HELEN: Eh? Oh! Yes, I did see a lad hanging around here when I called last week. Handsome, long-legged creature – just the way I like 'em. Perhaps he's one of the fixtures. He'd just do for you, Jo; you've never had a boy friend, have you?

JO: No. I used to like one of your fancy men though.

HELEN: Oh! Which one?

JO: I thought I was in love with him.

HELEN: Which one does she mean?

JO: I thought he was the only man I'd ever love in my life and then he ran off with that landlady's daughter.

HELEN: Oh! Him.

JO: And I cried myself to sleep for weeks.

HELEN: She was a silly cat if ever there was one. You should have seen her. Honest to God! She was a sight for sore eyes. I'll have to tell you about her too sometime.

JO: I saw him again one day, on the street.

HELEN: Did you?

JO: I couldn't believe my eyes. He was thin, weak-chinned, with a funny turned-up nose.

HELEN: It wasn't his nose I was interested in.

[*Tugboat heard.*]

JO: Can you smell that river?

HELEN: I can't smell a thing! I've got such a cold.

JO: What's that big place over there?

HELEN: The slaughterhouse. Where all the cows, sheep and pigs go in and all the beef, pork and mutton comes out.

JO: I wonder what it'll be like here in the summer. I bet it'll smell.

HELEN: This whole city smells. Eee, there's a terrible draught in here. Where's it coming from? Look at that! What a damn silly place to put a window. This place is cold enough, isn't it, without giving shelter to the four winds.

JO: Helen, stop sniffing. It sounds awful.

HELEN: I can't help it. You'd sniff if you had a cold like this. She's not got a bit of consideration in her. It's self all the time.

JO: I'm going to unpack my bulbs. I wonder where I can put them.

HELEN: I could tell you.

JO: They're supposed to be left in a cool, dark place.

HELEN: That's where we all end up sooner or later. Still, it's no use worrying, is it?

JO: I hope they bloom. Always before when I've tried to fix up a window box nothin's ever grown in it.

HELEN: Why do you bother?

JO: It's nice to see a few flowers, isn't it?

HELEN: Where did you get those bulbs?

JO: The Park. The gardener had just planted about two hundred. I didn't think he'd miss half a dozen.

HELEN: That's the way to do things. If you see something

you want, take it. That's my daughter for you. If you spent half as much time on me as you do on them fiddling bits of greenery I'd be a damn sight better off. Go and see if that kettle's boiling.

JO: See yourself. I've got to find somewhere for my bulbs.

HELEN: See yourself! Do everything yourself. That's what happens. You bring 'em up and they turn round and talk to you like that. I would never have dared talk to my mother like that when I was her age. She'd have knocked me into the middle of next week. Oh! my head. Whenever I walk, you know how it is! What a journey! I never realized this city was so big. Have we got any aspirins left, Jo?

JO: No. I dreamt about you last night, Helen.

HELEN: You're going to have a shocking journey to school each day, aren't you? It must be miles and miles.

JO: Not for much longer.

HELEN: Why, are you still set on leaving school at Christmas?

JO: Yes.

HELEN: What are you going to do?

JO: Get out of your sight as soon as I can get a bit of money in my pocket.

HELEN: Very wise too. But how are you going to get your money in the first place? After all, you're not very fond of work, are you?

JO: No. I take after you.

HELEN [looking at the aspidistra]: That's nice, isn't it? Puts me in mind of my first job, in a tatty little pub down Whit Lane. I thought it was wonderful . . . You know, playing the piano and all that; a real get-together at weekends. Everybody standing up and giving a song. I used to bring the house down with this one. [Sings.]

> I'd give the song birds to the wild wood
> I'd give the sunset to the blind

> And to the old folks I'd give the memory
> of the baby upon their knee.

[*To orchestra*]: Come on, vamp it in with me.

JO: You can't play to that. It's got no rhythm.

HELEN: Oh! They'd tear it up, wouldn't they? [*She sings another verse.*] It's nice though, isn't it?

JO: What would you say if I did something like that?

HELEN: I should have taken up singing – everybody used to tell me. What did you say?

JO: I said what would you say if I got a job in a pub?

HELEN: You can't sing, can you? Anyway, it's your life, ruin it your own way. It's a waste of time interfering with other people, don't you think so? It takes me all my time to look after myself, I know that.

JO: That's what you said, but really you think you could make a better job of it, don't you?

HELEN: What?

JO: Ruining my life. After all, you've had plenty of practice.

HELEN: Yes, give praise where praise is due, I always say. I certainly supervised my own downfall. Oh! This chair's a bit low, isn't it? Could do with a cushion.

JO: Anyway I'm not getting married like you did.

HELEN: Oh!

JO: I'm too young and beautiful for that.

HELEN: Listen to it! Still, we all have funny ideas at that age, don't we – makes no difference though, we all end up same way sooner or later. Anyway, tell me about this dream you had.

JO: What dream?

HELEN: You said you had a dream about me.

JO: Oh that! It was nothing much. I was standing in a garden and there were some policemen digging and guess what they found planted under a rosebush?

HELEN: You.

JO: No – you.

HELEN: Why, had we run short of cemetery space? Well, I've always said we should be used for manure when we're gone. Go and see to that coffee. I'm dying for a hot drink. This bloody cold! It's all over me. I'm sure it's 'flu – I suppose I'd better clear some of this stuff away. She wouldn't think. Well, they don't at that age, do they? Oh! It gets me right here when I try to do anything when I bend, you know. Have you ever had it? I was thinking of washing my hair tonight, but I don't think it's wise to . . Christ! what the hell's she got in here . . . sooner her than me . . . what's this? [*Seeing drawings.*] Hey, Jo, Jo, what's this?

JO: What's what?

HELEN: Did you do this?

JO: Put it down.

HELEN: I thought you said you weren't good at anything.

JO: It's only a drawing.

HELEN: It's very good. Did you show them this at school?

JO: I'm never at one school long enough to show them anything.

HELEN: That's my fault, I suppose.

JO: You will wander about the country.

HELEN: It's the gipsy in me. I didn't realize I had such a talented daughter. Look at that. It's good, isn't it?

JO: I'm not just talented, I'm geniused.

HELEN: I think I'll hang this on the wall somewhere. Now, where will it be least noticeable? Don't snatch. Have you no manners? What's these?

JO: Seif-portraits. Give 'em here.

HELEN: Self-portraits? Oh! Well, I suppose you've got to draw pictures of yourself, nobody else would. Hey! Is that supposed to be me?

JO: Yes.

HELEN: Don't I look a misery? They're very artistic though,

I must say. Have you ever thought of going to a proper art school and getting a proper training?

JO: It's too late.

HELEN: I'll pay. You're not stupid. You'll soon learn.

JO: I've had enough of school. Too many different schools and too many different places.

HELEN: You're wasting yourself.

JO: So long as I don't waste anybody else. Why are you so suddenly interested in me, anyway? You've never cared much before about what I was doing or what I was trying to do or the difference between them.

HELEN: I know, I'm a cruel, wicked woman.

JO: Why did we have to come here anyway? We were all right at the other place.

HELEN: I was fed up with the other place.

JO: You mean you're running away from somebody.

HELEN: You're asking for a bloody good hiding, lady. Just be careful. Oh! She'd drive you out of your mind. And my head's splitting. Splitting in two.

JO: What about me? Don't you think I get fed up with all this flitting about? Where's the bathroom? I'm going to have a bath.

HELEN: You're always bathing.

JO: I'm not like you. I don't wait until it becomes necessary before I have a good wash.

HELEN: You'll find the communal latrine and wash-house at the end of the passage. And don't throw your things about, this place is untidy enough as it is.

JO: That's all we do, live out of a travelling-bag.

HELEN: Don't worry, you'll soon be an independent working woman and free to go where you please.

JO: The sooner the better. I'm sick of you. You've made my life a misery. And stop sneezing your 'flu bugs all over me. I don't want to catch your cold.

HELEN: Oh! Get out of my sight. Go and have your bath.

JO: You can get your own coffee too. Why should I do anything for you? You never do anything for me.

[*Music. Enter* PETER, *a brash car salesman, cigar in mouth.*]

HELEN: Oh! My God! Look what the wind's blown in. What do you want?

PETER: Just passing by, you know. Thought I'd take a look at your new headquarters.

HELEN: Just passing . . . How did you find my address?

PETER: I found it. Did you think you could escape me, dear?

JO: So that's what she was running away from.

PETER: Who's this?

HELEN: My daughter.

PETER: Oh! Hello there. That puts another ten years on her.

JO: What's this one called?

HELEN: Smith.

JO: You told me not to trust men calling themselves Smith.

HELEN: Oh go and have your bath.

JO: I don't know where the bathroom is.

HELEN: It's in a little hole in the corridor.

JO: Is he staying?

PETER: Yes, I'm staying.

JO: Then I'll go for my bath later.

HELEN: What did you want to follow me here for?

PETER [*fumbling*]: You know what I want.

HELEN: Give over! Jo, go and see to that coffee! He would show up just when I've got her hanging round my neck.

PETER: Do what your mother tells you.

JO: Ordering me about like a servant! [*She goes.* PETER *makes another pass at* HELEN.] The kettle's not boiling. I suppose she hasn't told you about me.

PETER: Christ!

HELEN: Go and lay the table.

JO: No.

HELEN: Well, do something. Turn yourself into a bloody

termite and crawl into the wall or something, but make yourself scarce.

PETER: Get rid of her.

HELEN: I can't. Anyway, nobody asked you to come here.

PETER: Why did you come here? I had to chase all over town looking for you, only to finish up in this dump.

HELEN: Oh shut up! I've got a cold.

PETER: What on earth made you choose such a ghastly district?

HELEN: I can't afford to be so classy.

PETER: Tenements, cemetery, slaughterhouse.

HELEN: Oh we've got the lot here.

PETER: Nobody could live in a place like this.

JO: Only about fifty thousand people.

PETER: And a snotty-nosed daughter.

HELEN: I said nobody asked you to come. Oh my God! I'll have to have a dose of something. My head's swimming. Why did you?

PETER: Why did I what?

HELEN: Follow me here?

PETER: Now you know you're glad to see me, kid.

HELEN: No I'm not. The only consolation I can find in your immediate presence is your ultimate absence.

PETER: In that case, I'll stay.

HELEN: I warned you. I told you I was throwing my hand in. Now didn't I?

PETER: You did.

HELEN: Oh! Throw that cigar away. It looks bloody ridiculous stuck in your mouth like a horizontal chimney.

PETER: Your nose is damp. Here, have this.

HELEN: Oh go away!

PETER: Give it a good blow.

HELEN: Leave it alone.

PETER: Blow your nose, woman. [*She does.*] And while you're at it blow a few of those cobwebs out of your head. You can't afford to lose a man like me.

T.H.-B

HELEN: Can't I?

PETER: This is the old firm. You can't renege on the old firm.

HELEN: I'm a free lance. Besides, I'm thinking of giving it up.

PETER: What?

HELEN: Sex! Men!

PETER: What have we done to deserve this?

HELEN: It's not what you've done. It's what I've done.

PETER: But [*approaching her*], darling, you do it so well.

HELEN: Now give over, Peter. I've got all these things to unpack.

PETER: Send her to the pictures.

HELEN: I don't feel like it.

PETER: What's wrong?

HELEN: I'm tired. It's terrible when you've got a cold, isn't it? You don't fancy anything.

PETER: Well, put your hat on, let's go for a drink. Come on down to the church and I'll make an honest woman of you.

HELEN [*she goes to put her coat on, then changes her mind*]: No, I don't fancy it.

PETER: I'm offering to marry you, dear.

HELEN: You what?

PETER: Come on, let's go for a drink.

HELEN: I told you I don't fancy it.

PETER: You won't find anything better.

HELEN: Listen, love, I'm old enough to be your mother.

PETER [*petting her*]: Now you know I like this mother and son relationship.

HELEN: Stop it!

PETER: Aren't you wearing your girdle?

HELEN: Now, Peter.

PETER: Whoops!

HELEN: Well, you certainly liberate something in me. And I don't think it's maternal instincts either.

PETER [*sings*]: "Walter, Walter, lead me to the altar!"

HELEN: Some hopes.

PETER: Helen, you don't seem to realize what an opportunity I'm giving you. The world is littered with women I've rejected, women still anxious to indulge my little vices and excuse my less seemly virtues. Marry me, Helen. I'm young, good-looking and well set up. I may never ask you again.

HELEN: You're drunk.

PETER: I'm as sober as a judge.

HELEN: If you ask me again I might accept.

PETER [sings]: "I see a quiet place, a fireplace, a cosy room."

HELEN: Yes, the tap room at the Red Lion. What are you after?

PETER: You know what I like.

JO [coughs, enters]: Here's your coffee. Excuse me if I interrupted something. I'm sorry the crockery isn't very elegant, but it's all we've got.

PETER: Don't run away.

JO: I'm not running. [Sits.]

PETER: Is she always like this?

HELEN: She's jealous . . .

PETER: That's something I didn't bargain for.

HELEN: Can't bear to see me being affectionate with anybody.

JO: You've certainly never been affectionate with me.

PETER: Still, she's old enough to take care of herself. What sort of coffee is this anyway? It can hardly squeeze itself through the spout.

HELEN: She always does that. Makes it as weak as she can because she knows I like it strong. Don't drink that, it isn't worth drinking. Leave it.

JO: She should be in bed.

PETER: I know she should.

JO: You look very pale and sickly, Helen.

HELEN: Thank you.

JO: Is he going?

HELEN: Yes, come on, you'd better go before you catch my cold.

[*He pulls her to him as she passes.*]

PETER: Come outside then.

HELEN: No.

PETER: What does the little lady want? An engagement ring?

JO: I should have thought their courtship had passed the stage of symbolism.

HELEN: I always accept the odd diamond ring with pleasure.

PETER: I know it's my money you're after.

HELEN: Are you kidding?

JO: Hey!

[*He embraces* HELEN *at the door and begins to tell her a dirty story.*]

PETER: Did I ever tell you about the bookie who married the prostitute?

HELEN: No. Go on.

JO: Hey! What sort of a cigar is that?

PETER: Why don't you go home to your father?

JO: He's dead.

PETER: Too bad. Anyway, this bookie . . .

JO: Is it a Havana?

HELEN: Yes.

PETER: A rich, dark Havana, rolled on the thigh of a coal black mammy.

JO: You want to be careful. You never know where a coal black mammy's thigh's been.

HELEN: Take no notice of her. She think's she's funny.

JO: So does he! I bet he's married.

[HELEN *bursts out laughing at his joke.*)

You're not really going to marry her, are you? She's a devil with the men.

PETER: Are you, Helen?

HELEN: Well, I don't consider myself a slouch. Now come on then, if you've finished what you came for you'd better get going. We've all this to clear away before we go to bed.

PETER: Well, I won't be round tomorrow; the cat's been on the strawberries.

HELEN: Get going.

PETER: Don't forget me.

JO: Shall I withdraw while you kiss her good night?

HELEN: I'll kiss you good night in a minute, lady, and it really will be good night.

PETER: Well, take care of your mother while she's ailing, Jo. You know how fragile these old ladies are.

HELEN: Go on, get! [*Exit* PETER.] Well, I'm going to bed. We'll shift this lot tomorrow. There's always another day.

JO: It's dark out there now. I think I'll have my bath in the morning.

HELEN: Are you afraid of the dark?

JO: You know I am.

HELEN: You should try not to be.

JO: I do.

HELEN: And you're still afraid?

JO: Yes.

HELEN: Then you'll have to try a bit harder, won't you?

JO: Thanks. I'll do that. What's the bed like?

HELEN: Like a coffin only not half as comfortable.

JO: Have you ever tried a coffin?

HELEN: I dare say I will one day. I do wish we had a hot water bottle.

JO: You should have asked him to stay. It wouldn't be the first time I've been thrown out of my bed to make room for one of your . . .

HELEN: For God's sake shut up! Close your mouth for five minutes. And you can turn the light off and come to bed.

JO: Aren't we going to clear this lot up?

HELEN: No, it'll look all right in the dark.

JO: Yes, it's seen at its best, this room, in the dark.

HELEN: Everything is seen at its best in the dark – including me. I love it. Can't understand why you're so scared of it.

JO: I'm not frightened of the darkness outside. It's the darkness inside houses I don't like.

HELEN: Come on! Hey, Jo, what would you do if I told you I was thinking of getting married again?

JO: I'd have you locked up in an institution right away!

HELEN: Come on.

[*Music. Fade out.*]

SCENE TWO

JO *and her* BOY FRIEND, *a coloured naval rating, walking on the street. They stop by the door.*

JO: I'd better go in now. Thanks for carrying my books.

BOY: Were you surprised to see me waiting outside school?

JO: Not really.

BOY: Glad I came?

JO: You know I am.

BOY: So am I.

JO: Well, I'd better go in.

BOY: Not yet! Stay a bit longer.

JO: All right! Doesn't it go dark early? I like winter. I like it better than all the other seasons.

BOY: I like it too. When it goes dark early it gives me more time for – [*He kisses her.*]

JO: Don't do that. You're always doing it.

BOY: You like it.

JO: I know, but I don't want to do it all the time.

BOY: Afraid someone'll see us?

JO: I don't care.

BOY: Say that again.

JO: I don't care.

BOY: You mean it too. You're the first girl I've met who really didn't care. Listen, I'm going to ask you something. I'm a man of few words. Will you marry me?

JO: Well, I'm a girl of few words. I won't marry you but you've talked me into it.

BOY: How old are you?

JO: Nearly eighteen.

BOY: And you really will marry me?

JO: I said so, didn't I? You shouldn't have asked me if you were only kidding me up. [*She starts to go.*]

BOY: Hey! I wasn't kidding. I thought you were. Do you really mean it? You will marry me?

JO: I love you.

BOY: How do you know?

JO: I don't know why I love you but I do.

BOY: I adore you. [*Swinging her through the air.*]

JO: So do I. I can't resist myself.

BOY: I've got something for you.

JO: What is it? A ring!

BOY: This morning in the shop I couldn't remember what sort of hands you had, long hands, small hands or what. I stood there like a damn fool trying to remember what they felt like. [*He puts the ring on and kisses her hand.*] What will your mother say?

JO: She'll probably laugh.

BOY: Doesn't she care who her daughter marries?

JO: She's not marrying you, I am. It's got nothing to do with her.

BOY: She hasn't seen me.

JO: And when she does?

BOY: She'll see a coloured boy.

JO: No, whatever else she might be, she isn't prejudiced against colour. You're not worried about it, are you?

BOY: So long as you like it.

JO: You know I do.

BOY: Well, that's all that matters.

JO: When shall we get married?

BOY: My next leave? It's a long time, six months.

JO: It'll give us a chance to save a bit of money. Here, see . . .
this ring . . . it's too big; look, it slides about . . . And I
couldn't wear it for school anyway. I might lose it. Let's
go all romantic. Have you got a bit of string?

BOY: What for?

JO: I'm going to tie it round my neck. Come on, turn your
pockets out. Three handkerchiefs, a safety pin, a screw!
Did that drop out of your head? Elastic bands! Don't little
boys carry some trash. And what's this?

BOY: Nothing.

JO: A toy car! Does it go?

BOY: Hm hm!

JO: Can I try it? [*She does.*]

BOY: She doesn't even know how it works. Look, not like that.

[*He makes it go fast.*]

JO: I like that. Can I keep it?

BOY: Yes, take it, my soul and all, everything.

JO: Thanks. I know, I can use my hair ribbon for my ring. Do
it up for me.

BOY: Pretty neck you've got.

JO: Glad you like it. It's my schoolgirl complexion. I'd better
tuck this out of sight. I don't want my mother to see it.
She'd only laugh. Did I tell you, when I leave school this
week I start a part-time job in a bar? Then as soon as I get
a full-time job, I'm leaving Helen and starting up in a room
somewhere.

BOY: I wish I wasn't in the Navy.

JO: Why?

BOY: We won't have much time together.

JO: Well, we can't be together all the time and all the time there is wouldn't be enough.

BOY: It's a sad story, Jo. Once, I was a happy young man, not a care in the world. Now! I'm trapped into a barbaric cult . . .

JO: What's that? Mau-Mau?

BOY: Matrimony.

JO: Trapped! I like that! You almost begged me to marry you.

BOY: You led me on. I'm a trusting soul. Who took me down to that deserted football pitch?

JO: Who found the football pitch? I didn't even know it existed. And it just shows how often you must have been there, too . . . you certainly know where all the best spots are. I'm not going there again . . . It's too quiet. Anything might happen to a girl.

BOY: It almost did. You shameless woman!

JO: That's you taking advantage of my innocence.

BOY: I didn't take advantage. I had scruples.

JO: You would have done. You'd have gone as far as I would have let you and no scruples would have stood in your way.

BOY: You enjoyed it as much as I did.

JO: Shut up! This is the sort of conversation that can colour a young girl's mind.

BOY: Women never have young minds. They are born three thousand years old.

JO: Sometimes you look three thousand years old. Did your ancestors come from Africa?

BOY: No. Cardiff. Disappointed? Were you hoping to marry a man whose father beat the tom-tom all night?

JO: I don't care where you were born. There's still a bit of jungle in you somewhere. [*A siren is heard.*] I'm going in now, I'm hungry. A young girl's got to eat, you know.

BOY: Honey, you've got to stop eating. No more food, no more make-up, no more fancy clothes; we're saving up to get married.

JO: I just need some new clothes too. I've only got this one coat. I have to use it for school and when I go out with you. I do feel a mess.

BOY: You look all right to me

JO: Shall I see you tonight?

BOY: No, I got work to do.

JO: What sort of work?

BOY: Hard work, it involves a lot of walking.

JO: And a lot of walking makes you thirsty. I know, you're going drinking.

BOY: That's right. It's one of the lads' birthdays. I'll see you tomorrow.

JO· All right. I'll tell you what, I won't bother going to school and we can spend the whole day together. I'll meet you down by that ladies' hairdressing place.

BOY: The place that smells of cooking hair?

JO: Yes, about ten o'clock.

BOY: Okay, you're the boss.

JO: Good night.

BOY: Aren't you going to kiss me good night?

JO: You know I am. [*Kisses him.*] I like kissing you. Good night.

BOY: Good night.

JO: Dream of me.

BOY: I dreamt about you last night. Fell out of bed twice.

JO: You're in a bad way.

BOY: You bet I am. Be seeing you!

JO [*as she goes*]: I love you.

BOY: Why?

JO: Because you're daft.

[*He waves good-bye, turns and sings to the audience, and goes. HELEN dances on to the music, lies down and reads an evening paper. JO dances on dreamily.*]

HELEN: You're a bit late coming home from school, aren't you?

JO: I met a friend.

HELEN: Well, he certainly knows how to put stars in your eyes.

JO: What makes you think it's a he?

HELEN: Well, I certainly hope it isn't a she who makes you walk round in this state.

JO: He's a sailor.

HELEN: I hope you exercised proper control over his nautical ardour. I've met a few sailors myself.

JO: He's lovely.

HELEN: Is he?

JO: He's got beautiful brown eyes and gorgeous curly hair.

HELEN: Has he got long legs?

JO: They're all right.

HELEN: How old is he?

JO: Twenty-two. He's doing his national service, but before that he was a male nurse.

HELEN: A male nurse, eh? That's interesting. Where did he do his nursing?

JO: In a hospital, of course! Where else do they have nurses?

HELEN: Does he ever get any free samples? We could do with a few contacts for things like that.

JO: Oh shut up, Helen. Have a look in that paper and see what's on at the pictures tomorrow night.

HELEN: Where is it? Oh yes . . . *I was a Teenage* . . . what? You can't go there anyway, it's a proper little flea pit. *The Ten Commandments*, here, that'd do you good. *Desire Under the* . . . oh! What a funny place to have desire! You might as well have it at home as anywhere else, mightn't you? No, there's nothing here that I fancy.

JO: You never go to the pictures.

HELEN: I used to but the cinema has become more and more like the theatre, it's all mauling and muttering, can't hear what they're saying half the time and when you do it's not worth listening to. Look at that advertisement. It's pornographic. In my opinion such a frank and open display of the female form can only induce little boys of all ages to add vulgar comments in pencil. I ask you, what sort of an inflated woman is that? She's got bosom, bosom and still more bosom. I bet every inch of her chest is worth it's weight in gold. Let's have a look at you. I wonder if I could turn you into a mountain of voluptuous temptation?

JO: Why?

HELEN: I'd put you on films.

JO: I'd sooner be put on't streets. It's more honest.

HELEN: You might have to do that yet.

JO: Where did this magazine come from?

HELEN: Woman downstairs give it me.

JO: I didn't think you'd buy it.

HELEN: Why buy when it's cheaper to borrow?

JO: What day was I born on?

HELEN: I don't know.

JO: You should remember such an important event.

HELEN: I've always done my best to forget that.

JO: How old was I when your husband threw you out?

HELEN: Change the subject. When I think of her father and my husband it makes me wonder why I ever bothered, it does really.

JO: He was rich, wasn't he . . .

HELEN: He was a rat!

JO: He was your husband. Why did you marry him?

HELEN: At the time I had nothing better to do. Then he divorced me; that was your fault.

JO: I agree with him. If I was a man and my wife had a baby that wasn't mine I'd sling her out.

HELEN: Would you? It's a funny thing but I don't think I would. Still, why worry?

JO [reading from magazine]: It says here that Sheik Ahmed – an Arabian mystic – will, free of all charge, draw up for you a complete analysis of your character and destiny.

HELEN: Let's have a look.

JO: There's his photograph.

HELEN: Oh! He looks like a dirty little spiv. Listen Jo, don't bother your head about Arabian mystics. There's two w's in your future. Work or want, and no Arabian Knight can tell you different. We're all at the steering wheel of our own destiny. Careering along like drunken drivers. I'm going to get married. [*The news is received in silence.*] I said, I'm going to get married.

JO: Yes, I heard you the first time. What do you want me to do, laugh and throw pennies? Is it that Peter Smith?

HELEN: He's the unlucky man.

JO: You're centuries older than him.

HELEN: Only ten years.

JO: What use can a woman of that age be to anybody?

HELEN: I wish you wouldn't talk about me as if I'm an impotent, shrivelled old woman without a clue left in her head.

JO: You're not exactly a child bride.

HELEN: I have been one once, or near enough.

JO: Just imagine it, you're forty years old. I hope to be dead and buried before I reach that age. You've been living for forty years.

HELEN: Yes, it must be a biological phenomena.

JO: You don't look forty. You look a sort of well-preserved sixty.

[*Music. Enter* PETER *carrying a large bouquet and a box of chocolates and looking uncomfortable.*]

HELEN: Oh look, and it's all mine!

JO: Hello, Daddy.

PETER: Oh! So you told her.

HELEN. Of course. Come in and sit down. On second thoughts lie down, you look marvellous.

[*He gives her the bouquet.*]

Oh! really, you shouldn't have bothered yourself. I know

the thought was there, but . . . here, Jo, have we got a
vase, put these in some water.

JO: How did she talk you into it? You must be out of your
mind.

PETER: That's possible, I suppose.

JO: Flowers and all the trimmings. Helen can't eat anything
sweet and delicious. She's got to watch her figure.

HELEN: Nonsense! My figure hasn't altered since I was
eighteen.

JO: Really?

HELEN: Not an inch.

JO: I hope I'm luckier with mine.

HELEN: Do you see anything objectionable about my figure,
Peter?

PETER: I find the whole thing most agreeable.

JO: You've got to say that, you're marrying it!

PETER: The chocolates are for you, Jo.

JO: Buying my silence, hey? It's a good idea. I like chocolates.

HELEN: Help yourself to a drink, Peter, and I'll go and put my
glad rags on. [*Exit.*]

PETER: Don't let's be long, huh? I've booked a table. Dammit,
I thought you'd be ready.

JO: She's got no sense of time.

PETER: Don't sit there guzzling all those chocolates at once.
[*She throws the lid at him.*]
What the hell are you playing at . . . sit down and behave
yourself, you little snip.

JO: Hey! Don't start bossing me about. You're not my father.

PETER. Christ Almighty! Will you sit down and eat your
chocolates. Do what you like but leave me alone.
[*Suddenly she attacks him, half-laughing, half-crying.*]

JO: You leave me alone. And leave my mother alone too.
[HELEN *enters.*]

PETER: Get away! For God's sake go and . . .

HELEN: Leave him alone, Jo. He doesn't want to be bothered

with you. Got a cigarette, Peter? Did you get yourself a drink?

PETER: No, I . . .

JO: Do I bother you, Mister Smith, or must I wait till we're alone for an answer?

PETER: Can't you keep her under control?

HELEN: I'll knock her head round if she isn't careful. Be quiet, Jo. And don't tease him.

PETER: Tonight's supposed to be a celebration.

JO: What of?

HELEN: He's found a house. Isn't he marvellous? Show her the photo of it, Peter. I shan't be a tick!

JO: You've certainly fixed everything up behind my back.

HELEN: Don't you think it's nice? One of his pals had to sell moving into something smaller. [*Goes.*]

[PETER *throws snap on to the table.*]

JO: It's not bad. White walls, tennis courts. Has it got a swimming pool?

PETER: It has twelve swimming pools.

JO: Can I see the other photos?

PETER: Which photos?

JO: In your wallet. I suppose you thought I didn't notice.

PETER: Oh! These. Yes, well, that's a photograph of my family, my mother, my father, my sister, my brother and . . . [*To himself.*] all the rest of the little bastards.

JO: Is this a wedding group?

PETER: My brother's wedding.

JO: They only just made it, too, from the look of his wife. You can tell she's going to have a baby.

PETER: Oh? Thank you.

JO: You can have it back if I can see the others.

PETER: Which others? What are you talking about?

JO: Do you want me to tell my mother?

PETER: I don't give a damn what you tell your mother.

JO: They're all women, aren't they? I bet you've had thousands of girl friends. What was this one with the long legs called?

PETER: Ah! Yes, number thirty-eight. A charming little thing.

JO: Why do you wear that black patch?

PETER: I lost an eye.

JO: Where?

PETER: During the war.

JO: Were you in the Navy?

PETER: Army.

JO: Officer?

PETER: Private.

JO: I thought you would have been somebody very important.

PETER: A private is far more important than you think. After all, who does all the dirty work?

JO: Yes, a general without any army wouldn't be much use, would he? Can I see your eye? I mean can I see the hole?

PETER: There's nothing to see.

JO: Do you wear that patch when you go to bed?

PETER: That's something about which I don't care to make a public statement.

JO: Tell me.

PETER: Well, there is one highly recommended way for a young girl to find out.

JO [*glancing through photos in wallet*]: I don't like this one. She's got too much stuff on her eyes.

PETER: That's the sort of thing your sex goes in for.

JO: I don't. I let my natural beauty shine through.

PETER: Is there no alternative?

JO: Don't you like shiny faces?

PETER: I suppose they're all right on sweet young things but I just don't go for sweet young things –

JO: Do you fancy me?

PETER: Not yet.

JO: You prefer old women.

PETER: She isn't old.

JO: She soon will be.

PETER: Ah well, that's love. [*Sings.*] "That wild, destructive thing called love."

JO: Why are you marrying Helen?

PETER: Why shouldn't I marry Helen?

JO: Your generation has 'some very peculiar ideas, that's all I can say.

PETER: Could I have my photographs back, please?

JO: There . . .

PETER: You don't like your mother much do you?

JO: She doesn't much care for me either.

PETER: I can understand that.

JO [*looking over his shoulder at photographs*]: I like that one with the shaggy hair cut. She's got nice legs too. Nearly as nice as mine.

PETER: Would you care for a smoke?

JO: Thanks.

[HELEN *is heard singing off stage*]:

HELEN: Jo! Where's my hat?

JO: I don't know. Where you left it. It's no use getting impatient, Peter. The art work takes a long time. Are you sure you lost your eye during the war? What happened?

PETER: Go and tell your mother I'll wait for her in the pub.

JO: Are you married?

PETER [*going*]: No, I'm still available.

HELEN [*entering*]: But only just.

PETER: Helen, you look utterly fantastic.

HELEN: Thanks. Put that cigarette out, Jo, you've got enough bad habits without adding to your repertoire. Do you like my hat, Peter?

PETER: Bang-on, darling!

HELEN: What are all these books doing all over the place? Are you planning a moonlight flit, Jo? Stop it, Peter.

T.H.–C

PETER: Got your blue garters on?

HELEN: Now, Peter. Come on, Jo, shift these books.

JO: I'm sorting them.

PETER [*taking* HELEN'S *hat*]: How do I look?

HELEN: Peter!

JO: Have you forgotten I'm leaving school this week?

HELEN: Peter, give it here. Stop fooling about. It took me ages
    to get this hat on right. Jo, do as you're told.

JO: All right.

HELEN: Peter! Don't do that. Give it to me. It's my best one.
    Put it down.

PETER [*to himself*]: No bloody sense of humour.

HELEN: What has she got here? Look at 'em. *Selected Nursery
    Rhymes*, Hans Andersen's *Fairy Tales*, *Pinocchio*. Well,
    you certainly go in for the more advanced types of litera-
    ture. And what's this? The Holy Bible!

JO: You ought to read it. I think it's good.

HELEN: The extent of my credulity always depends on the
    extent of my alcoholic intake. Eat, drink and be merry –

JO: And live to regret it.

PETER: God! We've got a founder member of the Lord's Day
    Observance Society here.

JO: What are you marrying him for?

HELEN: He's got a wallet full of reasons.

JO: Yes. I've just seen 'em too.

HELEN: Can you give us a quid, Peter? I'd better leave her
    some money. We might decide to have a weekend at
    Blackpool and she can't live on grass and fresh air.

JO: I won't set eyes on her for a week now. I know her when
    she's in the mood. What are you going to do about me,
    Peter? The snotty-nosed daughter? Don't you think I'm
    a bit young to be left like this on my own while you flit
    off with my old woman?

PETER: She'll be all right, won't she? At her age.

HELEN: We can't take her with us. We will be, if you'll not take exception to the phrase, on our honeymoon. Unless we change our minds.

PETER: I'm not having her with us.

HELEN: She can stay here then. Come on. I'm hungry.

JO: So am I.

HELEN: There's plenty of food in the kitchen.

JO: You should prepare my meals like a proper mother.

HELEN: Have I ever laid claim to being a proper mother? If you're too idle to cook your own meals you'll just have to cut food out of your diet altogether. That should help you lose a bit of weight, if nothing else.

PETER: She already looks like a bad case of malnutrition.

JO: Have you got your key, Helen? I might not be here when you decide to come back. I'm starting work on Saturday.

HELEN: Oh yes, she's been called to the bar.

PETER: What sort of a bar?

JO: The sort you're always propping up. I'm carrying on the family traditions. Will you give me some money for a new dress, Helen?

HELEN: If you really want to make a good investment, you'll buy a needle and some cotton. Every article of clothing on her back is held together by a safety pin or a knot. If she had an accident in the street I'd be ashamed to claim her.

PETER: Are we going?

JO: Can't I come with you?

HELEN: Shut up! You're going to have him upset. You jealous little cat! Come on, Peter.

PETER: All right, all right, don't pull. Don't get excited. And don't get impatient. Those bloody little street kids have probably pulled the car to pieces by now but we needn't worry about that, need we . . .

HELEN: I told you you'd upset him.

PETER: Upset? I'm not upset. I just want to get to hell out of this black hole of Calcutta.

[*They leave flat.* JO *looks after them for a moment then turns to bed – she lies across it, crying. Music.* BLACK BOY *enters.*]

BOY [*calling*]: Jo!

[*She doesn't move.*]

BOY: Joee!

JO: Coming.

[*They move towards each other as if dancing to the music. The music goes, the lights change.*]

JO: Oh! It's you! Come in. Just when I'm feeling and looking a mess.

BOY: What's wrong? You been crying?

JO: No.

BOY: You have. Your eyes are red.

JO: I don't cry. I've got a cold.

BOY: I think you have, too. Yes, you've got a bit of a temperature. Have you been eating?

JO: No.

BOY: You're a fine sight. Where's the kitchen?

JO: Through there. What are you going to do?

BOY: Fix you a cold cure. Where do you keep the milk?

JO: Under the sink. I hate milk.

BOY: I hate dirt. And this is just the dirtiest place I've ever seen. The children round here are filthy.

JO: It's their parents' fault. What are you putting in that milk?

BOY: A pill.

JO: I bet it's an opium pellet. I've heard about men like you.

BOY: There isn't another man like me anywhere. I'm one on his own.

JO: So am I.

BOY: Who was that fancy bit I saw stepping out of here a few minutes ago?

JO: If she was dressed up like Hope Gardens it was my mother.

BOY: And who is the Pirate King?

JO: She's marrying him. Poor devil!

BOY: You'll make a pretty bridesmaid.

JO: Bridesmaid! I'd sooner go to my own funeral.

BOY: You'd better drink this first.

JO: I don't like it.

BOY: Get it down you.

JO: But look, it's got skin on the top.

BOY: Don't whine. I'm not spending the evening with a running-nosed wreck. Finish your milk.

JO: Did you treat your patients in hospital like this?

BOY: Not unless they were difficult. Your mother looks very young, Jo, to have a daughter as old as you.

JO: She can still have children.

BOY: Well, that's an interesting bit of news. Why should I worry if she can have children or not?

JO: Do you fancy her?

BOY: That isn't the sort of question you ask your fiancé.

JO: It doesn't really matter if you do fancy her, anyway, because she's gone. You're too late. You've had your chips.

BOY: I'll be gone soon, too. What then?

JO: My heart's broke.

BOY: You can lie in bed at night and hear my ship passing down the old canal. It's cold in here. No fire?

JO: It doesn't work.

BOY: Come and sit down here. You can keep me warm.

JO: Is it warm where you're going?

BOY: I guess so.

JO: We could do with a bit of sunshine. In this country there are only two seasons, winter and winter. Do you think Helen's beautiful?

BOY: Who's Helen?

JO: My mother. Honestly, you are slow sometimes. Well, do you think she's beautiful?

BOY: Yes.

JO: Am I like her?

BOY: No, you're not at all like her.

JO: Good. I'm glad nobody can see a resemblance between us.

BOY: My ring's still round your neck. Wear it. Your mother isn't here to laugh.

JO: Unfasten it, then.

BOY: Pretty neck you've got.

JO: Glad you like it.

BOY: No! Let me put it on.

JO: Did it cost very much?

BOY: You shouldn't ask questions like that. I got it from Woolworths!

JO: Woolworth's best! I don't care. I'm not proud. It's the thought that counts and I wonder what thought it was in your wicked mind that made you buy it.

BOY· I've got dishonourable intentions.

JO: I'm so glad.

BOY: Are you? [*He embraces her.*]

JO: Stop it.

BOY: Why? Do you object to the "gross clasps of the lascivious Moor"?

JO: Who said that?

BOY: Shakespeare in *Othello*.

JO: Oh! Him. He said everything, didn't he?

BOY: Let me be your Othello and you my Desdemona.

JO: All right.

BOY: "Oh ill-starred wench."

JO: Will you stay here for Christmas?

BOY: If that's what you want.

JO: It's what you want.

BOY: That's right.

JO: Then stay.

BOY: You naughty girl!

JO: I may as well be naughty while I've got the chance. I'll probably never see you again. I know it.

BOY: What makes you say that?

JO: I just know it. That's all. But I don't care. Stay with me

now, it's enough, it's all I want, and if you do come back
I'll still be here.

BOY: You think I'm only after one thing, don't you?

JO: I know you're only after one thing.

BOY: You're so right. [*He kisses her.*] But I will come back. I
love you.

JO: How can you say that?

BOY: Why or how I say these things I don't know, but whatever it means it's true.

JO: Anyway, after this you might not want to come back. After
all, I'm not very experienced in these little matters.

BOY: I am.

JO: Anyway, it's a bit daft for us to be talking about you
coming back before you've gone. Can I leave that hot
milk?

BOY: It would have done you good. Never mind. [*Embraces
her.*]

JO: Don't do that.

BOY: Why not?

JO: I like it.

[*Fade out. Music. Wedding bells.* HELEN'S *music. She dances
on with an assortment of fancy boxes, containing her wedding
clothes.*]

HELEN: Jo! Jo! Come on. Be sharp now.

[JO *comes on in her pyjamas. She has a heavy cold.*]

For God's sake give me a hand. I'll never be ready. What
time is it? Have a look at the church clock.

JO: A quarter past eleven, and the sun's coming out

HELEN: Oh! Well, happy the bride the sun shines on.

JO: Yeah, and happy the corpse the rain rains on. You're not
getting married in a church, are you?

HELEN: Why, are you coming to throw bricks at us? Of
course not. Do I look all right? Pass me my fur. Oh! My
fur! Do you like it?

JO: I bet somebody's missing their cat.

HELEN: It's a wedding present from that young man of mine. He spends his money like water, you know, penny wise, pound foolish. Oh! I am excited. I feel twenty-one all over again. Oh! You would have to catch a cold on my wedding day. I was going to ask you to be my bridesmaid too.

JO: Don't talk daft.

HELEN: Where did you put my shoes? Did you clean 'em? Oh! They're on my feet. Don't stand there sniffing, Jo. Use a handkerchief.

JO: I haven't got one.

HELEN: Use this, then. What's the matter with you? What are you trying to hide?

JO: Nothing.

HELEN: Don't try to kid me. What is it? Come on, let's see.

JO: It's nothing. Let go of me. You're hurting.

HELEN: What's this?

JO: A ring.

HELEN: I can see it's a ring. Who give it to you?

JO: A friend of mine.

HELEN: Who? Come on. Tell me.

JO: You're hurting me.

[HELEN *breaks the cord and gets the ring.*]

HELEN: You should have sewn some buttons on your pyjamas if you didn't want me to see. Who give it you?

JO: My boy friend. He asked me to marry him.

HELEN: Well, you silly little bitch. You mean that lad you've been knocking about with while we've been away?

JO: Yes.

HELEN: I could choke you.

JO: You've already had a damn good try.

HELEN: You haven't known him five minutes. Has he really asked you to marry him?

JO: Yes.

HELEN: Well, thank God for the divorce courts! I suppose just because I'm getting married you think you should.

JO: Have you got the monopoly?

HELEN: You stupid little devil! What sort of a wife do you think you'd make? You're useless. It takes you all your time to look after yourself. I suppose you think you're in love. Anybody can fall in love, do you know that? But what do you know about the rest of it?

JO: Ask yourself.

HELEN: You know where that ring should be? In the ashcan with everything else. Oh! I could kill her, I could really.

JO: You don't half knock me about. I hope you suffer for it.

HELEN: I've done my share of suffering if I never do any more. Oh Jo, you're only a kid. Why don't you learn from my mistakes? It takes half your life to learn from your own.

JO: You leave me alone. Can I have my ring back, please?

HELEN: What a thing to happen just when I'm going to enjoy myself for a change.

JO: Nobody's stopping you.

HELEN: Yes, and as soon as my back's turned you'll be off with this sailor boy and ruin yourself for good.

JO: I'm already ruined.

HELEN: Yes, it's just the sort of thing you'd do. You make me sick.

JO: You've no need to worry, Helen. He's gone away. He may be back in six months, but there again, he may . . .

HELEN: Look, you're only young. Enjoy your life. Don't get trapped. Marriage can be hell for a kid.

JO: Can I have your hanky back?

HELEN: Where did you put it?

JO: This is your fault too.

HELEN: Everything's my fault. Show me your tongue.

JO: Breathing your 'flu bugs all over me.

HELEN: Yes, and your neck's red where I pulled that string.

JO: Will you get me a drink of water, Helen?

HELEN: No, have a dose of this [*Offering whisky.*] It'll do you more good. I might as well have one myself while I'm at it, mightn't I?

JO: You've emptied more bottles down your throat in the last few weeks than I would have thought possible. If you don't watch it, you'll end up an old down-and-out boozer knocking back the meths.

HELEN: It'll never come to that. The devil looks after his own, they say.

JO: He certainly takes good care of you. You look marvellous, considering.

HELEN: Considering what?

JO: The wear and tear on your soul.

HELEN: Oh well, that'll have increased its market value, won't it?

JO: Old Nick'll get you in the end.

HELEN: Thank God for that! Heaven must be the hell of a place. Nothing but repentant sinners up there, isn't it? All the pimps, prostitutes and politicians in creation trying to cash in on eternity and their little tin god. Where's my hat?

JO: Where's your husband?

HELEN: Probably drunk with his pals somewhere. He was going down to the house this morning to let some air in. Have you seen a picture of the house? Yes, you have. Do you like it? [*She peers and primps into mirror.*]

JO: It's all right if you like that sort of thing, and I don't.

HELEN: I'll like it in a few years, when it isn't so new and clean. At the moment it's like my face, unblemished! Oh look at that, every line tells a dirty story, hey?

JO: Will you tell me something before you go?

HELEN: Oh! You can read all about that in books.

JO: What was my father like?

[HELEN *turns away.*]

HELEN: Who?

JO: You heard! My father! What was he like?

HELEN: Oh! Him.

JO: Well, was he so horrible that you can't even tell me about him?

HELEN: He wasn't horrible. He was just a bit stupid, you know. Not very bright.

JO: Be serious, Helen.

HELEN: I am serious.

JO: Are you trying to tell me he was an idiot?

HELEN: He wasn't an idiot, he was just a bit – retarded.

JO: You liar!

HELEN: All right, I'm a liar.

JO: Look at me.

HELEN: Well, am I?

JO: No.

HELEN: Well, now you know.

JO: How could you give me a father like that?

HELEN: I didn't do it on purpose. How was I to know you'd materialize out of a little love affair that lasted five minutes?

JO: You never think. That's your trouble.

HELEN: I know.

JO: Was he like a . . . a real idiot?

HELEN: I've told you once. He was nice though, you know, a nice little feller!

JO: Where is he now, locked up?

HELEN: No, he's dead.

JO: Why?

HELEN: Why? Well, I mean, death's something that comes to us all, and when it does come you haven't usually got time to ask why.

JO: It's hereditary, isn't it?

HELEN: What?

JO: Madness

HELEN: Sometimes.

JO: Am I mad?

HELEN: Decide for yourself. Oh, Jo, don't be silly. Of course you're not daft. Not more so than anybody else.

JO: Why did you have to tell me that story? Couldn't you have made something up?

HELEN: You asked for the truth and you got it for once. Now be satisfied.

JO: How could you go with a half-wit?

HELEN: He had strange eyes. You've got 'em. Everybody used to laugh at him. Go on, I'll tell you some other time.

JO: Tell me now!

HELEN: Mind my scent!

JO: Please tell me. I want to understand.

HELEN: Do you think I understand? For one night, actually it was the afternoon, I loved him. It was the first time I'd ever really been with a man . . .

JO: You were married.

HELEN: I was married to a Puritan – do you know what I mean?

JO: I think so.

HELEN: And when I met your father I was as pure and un-sullied as I fondly, and perhaps mistakenly, imagine you to be. It was the first time and though you can enjoy the second, the third, even the fourth time, there's no time like the first, it's always there. I'm off now. I've got to go and find my husband. Now don't sit here sulking all day.

JO: I was thinking.

HELEN: Well, don't think. It doesn't do you any good. I'll see you when the honeymoon's over. Come on, give us a kiss. You may as well. It's a long time since you kissed me.

JO: Keep it for him.

HELEN: I don't suppose you're sorry to see me go.

JO: I'm not sorry and I'm not glad.

HELEN: You don't know what you do want.

JO: Yes, I do. I've always known what I want.

HELEN: And when it comes your way will you recognize it?

JO: Good luck, Helen.

HELEN: I'll be seeing you. Hey! If he doesn't show up I'll be
    back.
JO: Good luck, Helen.

[*Exit* HELEN. *"Here comes the Bride"* *on the cornet.*]

Curtain.

Act Two

SCENE ONE

As the curtain goes up fairground music can be heard in the distance. JO *and a boy can be heard playing together. When they enter the flat they have been playing about with a bunch of brightly coloured balloons. It is summer now and* JO'S *pregnancy is quite obvious.*

JO [*as she falls on a couch in the darkened room*]: Let me lie here and don't wake me up for a month.

GEOF: Shall I put the light on?

JO: No. Don't you dare put that light on.

GEOF: Did you enjoy the fair?

JO: Loved it. I haven't been to a fair since Christmas.

GEOF: Those roundabouts are still going. Can you hear 'em?

JO: I should be up at half past seven tomorrow morning. I'll never make it. I'll just have to be late. Anyway, why should I slave away for anybody but me? Haven't you got a home to go to, Geof?

GEOF: Of course.

JO: Well, why are you lurking about? Come in if you want to.

GEOF: Thanks.

JO: There's some biscuits and a flask of coffee in the kitchen only I'm too tired to get 'em. Aren't you hungry?

GEOF: No, but you are.

JO: That's right. Go and get 'em for me, Geof.

GEOF: Where's the kitchen?

JO: Straight on.

GEOF: I'll put the light on.

JO: No, you won't! I like this romantic half-light, it just goes with this Manchester maisonette!

GEOF: Take four paces forward, turn right, turn left, once round the gasworks and straight on up the creek. [*He bangs into a chair or table and cries or swears.*]

JO: Put a match on, you daft thing.

[GEOF *strikes a match.*]

GEOF: Ee, this place is enormous, isn't it?

JO: I know. I've got to work all day in a shoe shop and all night in a bar to pay for it. But it's mine. All mine.

GEOF: I can tell it's yours from the state it's in. No wonder you won't put the light on. Where do you keep the cups?

JO: In the sink.

GEOF: Isn't this place a bit big for one, Jo?

JO: Why? Are you thinking of moving in?

GEOF: Not likely.

JO: You are, you know. Put 'em down here. Don't you want any?

GEOF: No.

JO: Well, hand 'em over to me because I'm starved. Has your landlady thrown you out?

GEOF: Don't be silly.

JO: I've been wondering why you were so anxious to see me home. You didn't fancy sleeping under the arches, did you? Why did your landlady throw you out, Geoffrey? I'll let you stay here if you tell me.

GEOF: I was behind with the rent.

JO: That's a lie for a start.

GEOF: I don't tell lies.

JO: Come on, let's have some truth. Why did she throw you out?

GEOF: I've told you why.

JO [*switches on light*]: Come on, the truth. Who did she find you with? Your girl friend? It wasn't a man, was it?

GEOF: Don't be daft.

JO: Look, I've got a nice comfortable couch, I've even got some sheets. You can stay here if you'll tell me what you do. Go on, I've always wanted to know about people like you.

GEOF: Go to hell.

JO: I won't snigger, honest I won't. Tell me some of it, go on. I bet you never told a woman before.

GEOF: I don't go in for sensational confessions.

JO: I want to know what you do. I want to know why you do it. Tell me or get out.

GEOF: Right! [*He goes to the door.*]

JO: Geof, don't go. Don't go, Geof! I'm sorry. Please stay.

GEOF: Don't touch me.

JO: I didn't mean to hurt your feelings.

GEOF: I can't stand women at times. Let go of me.

JO: Come on, Geof. I don't care what you do.

GEOF: Thank you. May I go now, please?

JO: Please stay here Geof. I'll get those sheets and blankets.

GEOF: I can't stand people who laugh at other people. They'd get a bigger laugh if they laughed at themselves.

JO: Please stay, Geof. (*She goes off for the sheets and blankets. He finds her book of drawings on the table and glances through them.*]

GEOF: Are these yours?

JO: No, why? Put them down, Geof.

GEOF: Obviously they are. They're exactly like you.

JO: How do you mean?

GEOF: Well, there's no design, rhythm or purpose.

JO: Hey?

GEOF: Where's the design in that? It's all messy, isn't it? Charcoal. I don't like it.

JO: I do.

GEOF: What made you choose that for a subject?

JO: I like . . .

GEOF: They're all sentimental.

JO: Me? Sentimental?

GEOF: No. No. I don't like 'em.

JO: Do you really think they're sentimental?

GEOF: Well, look. I mean . . .

JO: I'm sorry you don't like them.

GEOF: Why don't you go to a decent school?

JO: I've never been to any school.

GEOF: You want taking in hand.

JO: No, thanks.

GEOF: Has anybody ever tried?

JO: What?

GEOF: Taking you in hand.

JO: Yes.

GEOF: What happened to him?

JO: He came in with Christmas and went out with the New
    Year.

GEOF: Did you like him?

JO: He was all right . . .

GEOF: Did you love him?

JO: I don't know much about love. I've never been too familiar
    with it. I suppose I must have loved him. They say love
    creates. And I'm certainly creating at the moment. I'm
    going to have a baby.

GEOF: I thought so. You're in a bit of a mess, aren't you?

JO: I don't care.

GEOF: You can get rid of babies before they're born, you know.

JO: I know, but I think that's terrible.

GEOF: When's it due?

JO: Reckon it up from Christmas.

GEOF: About September.

JO: Yes.

GEOF: What are you going to do? You can't be on your own.

JO: There's plenty of time.

GEOF: Got any money?

JO: Only my wages and they don't last long. By the time I've

T.H.–D

bought all I need, stockings and make-up and things, I've got nothing left.

GEOF: You can do without make-up.

JO: I can't. I look like a ghost without it.

GEOF: At your age?

JO: What's age got to do with it? Anyway, I'm not working for much longer. I'm not having everybody staring at me.

GEOF: How are you going to manage then?

JO: There's no need for you to worry about it.

GEOF: Somebody's got to. Anyway, I like you.

JO: I like you too.

GEOF: Your mother should know.

JO: Why?

GEOF: Well, she's your mother. Do you know her address?

JO: No. She was supposed to be marrying some man. They live in a big, white house somewhere.

GEOF: What sort of a woman is she?

JO: She's all sorts of woman. But she's got plenty of money.

GEOF: That's all you need to be interested in. You've got to buy all sorts of things for the baby. Clothes, a cot and a pram. Here, that teddy bear we won tonight'll come in handy, won't it? I can make things too. I'll help . . .

JO: Shut up! I'm not planning big plans for this baby, or dreaming big dreams. You know what happens when you do things like that. The baby'll be born dead or daft!

GEOF: You're feeling a bit depressed, Jo.

JO: I'm feeling nothing.

GEOF: You'll be your usual self soon.

JO: And what is my usual self? My usual self is a very unusual self, Geoffrey Ingram, and don't you forget it. I'm an extraordinary person. There's only one of me like there's only one of you.

GEOF: We're unique!

JO: Young.

GEOF: Unrivalled!

JO: Smashing!

GEOF: We're bloody marvellous!

JO: Hey! Do you like beer?

GEOF: Yes.

JO: Whisky?

GEOF: Yes.

JO: Gin?

GEOF: Yes. Have you got some?

JO: No, but if I had I'd give it all to you. I'd give everything
    I had to you. Here, have a biscuit. You'll like these. They
    taste like dog food.

GEOF: Spratts!

JO: You look like a spratt. Jack Spratt, who'd eat no fat, his
    wife would eat no lean and so between them both, you see,
    they licked the platter clean. Did you enjoy that dramatic
    recitation?

GEOF: Very moving.

JO: You say one.

GEOF: There was a young man of Thessaly,
      And he was wondrous wise.
      He jumped into a quickset hedge
      And scratched out both his eyes.
      And when he saw his eyes were out,
      With all his might and main
      He jumped into another hedge
      And scratched them in again.

JO: I like that. Do you know any more?

GEOF: As I was going up Pippin Hill,
      Pippin Hill was dirty.
      And there I met a pretty miss
      And she dropped me a curtsy.
      Little miss, pretty miss,
      Blessings light upon you.
      If I had half a crown a day
      I'd gladly spend it on you.

JO: Would you?

GEOF: I would.

JO: Silly things nursery rhymes when you weigh them up.

GEOF: I like them. Do you want a cigarette?

JO: How many have you got left?

GEOF: I've got enough for one each.

JO: No, you keep 'em. They don't bother me really. I used to smoke just to annoy my mother. What's that?

GEOF: A free gift coupon.

JO: Everything you buy lately has a free gift coupon in it. It's coming to something when they have to bribe the public to buy their stuff. What's this one for?

GEOF: There's a whole list of things to send for if you have enough coupons. Hee, there's even a car, smoke forty thousand cigarettes a day for the next ten thousand years and you'll get a Lagonda.

JO: What's that?

GEOF: A car.

JO: A nice car?

GEOF: A wonderful car.

JO: I'll buy you one for Christmas. If you ask me nice I'll buy you two.

GEOF: Thanks.

JO: Oh! I'm tired. This couch isn't going to be very comfortable, is it?

GEOF: It'll do.

JO: What are you going to sleep in?

GEOF: My shirt!

JO: I'm that tired! I haven't the energy to get myself to bed. You won't sleep very well on this couch, Geof.

GEOF: It's all right. Beggars can't be choosers.

JO: We're both beggars. A couple of degenerates.

GEOF: The devil's own!

JO [she goes to bed. GEOF starts to undress]: Hey! You'd better turn that light out, or I might be after you. [He turns the

*light out and then gets into bed. She begins to sing the song
"Black Boy" as she lies on her bed.*]
Black boy, black boy, don't you lie to me.
Where did you stay last night?
In the pines, in the pines where the sun never shines,
I shivered the whole night through.

GEOF: Jo!

JO: Yes.

GEOF: What was that boy like?

JO: Which boy?

GEOF: You know.

JO: Oh! Him. He wasn't a bit like you. He could sing and
dance and he was as black as coal.

GEOF: A black boy?

JO: From darkest Africa! A Prince.

GEOF: A what?

JO: A Prince, son of a chieftain.

GEOF: I'll bet he was too.

JO: Prince Ossini!

GEOF: What was he doing here?

JO: He was a male nurse in the Navy.

GEOF: Do you wish he was still here?

JO: Not really. I think I've had enough. I'm sick of love. That's
why I'm letting you stay here. You won't start anything.

GEOF: No, I don't suppose I will.

JO: You'd better not. I hate love.

GEOF: Do you, Jo?

JO: Yes, I do.

GEOF: Good night.

JO: Good night.

GEOF: You needn't lock the bedroom door.

JO: I'm in bed. Geoffrey! Geoffrey!

GEOF: What do you want?

JO: What time have you got to be up in the morning?

GEOF: I don't go to school tomorrow. I'll stay here and clear this place up a bit. And make you a proper meal. Now go to sleep, hey?

JO: Geoffrey!

GEOF: What's wrong now?

JO [*laughing*]: You're just like a big sister to me.

[*Music to black out. Then quick as lights go up. Waking,* GEOF *dances and goes off with bedclothes.* JO *dances off.* GEOF *dances in with props for the next scene, which in reality would be a month or two later.* GEOF *is cutting out a baby's gown.* JO *wanders about the room.*]

JO: God! It's hot.

GEOF: I know it's hot.

JO: I'm so restless.

GEOF: Oh, stop prowling about.

JO: This place stinks. [*Goes over to the door. Children are heard singing in the street.*] That river, it's the colour of lead. Look at that washing, it's dirty, and look at those filthy children.

GEOF: It's not their fault.

JO: It's their parents' fault. There's a little boy over there and his hair, honestly, it's walking away. And his ears. Oh! He's a real mess! He never goes to school. He just sits on that front doorstep all day. I think he's a bit deficient.

[*The children's voices die away. A tugboat hoots.*]

His mother ought not to be allowed.

GEOF: Who?

JO: His mother. Think of all the harm she does, having children.

GEOF. Sit down and read a book, Jo.

JO: I can't.

GEOF: Be quiet then. You're getting on my nerves. [*Suddenly she yells and whirls across the room.*]

JO: Wheee! Come on rain. Come on storm. It kicked me, Geof. It kicked me!

GEOF: What?

JO: It kicked me. [GEOF *runs to her and puts his head on her belly.*]

GEOF: Will it do it again?

JO: It shows it's alive anyway. Come on, baby, let's see what big sister's making for us.

GEOF: Put it down.

JO: What a pretty little dress.

GEOF: It's got to wear something. You can't just wrap it up in a bundle of newspaper.

JO: And dump it on a doorstep. How did Geoffrey find out the measurements?

GEOF: Babies are born to the same size more or less.

JO: Oh, no, they're not. Some are thin scrappy things and others are huge and covered in rolls of fat.

GEOF: Shut up, Jo, it sounds revolting.

JO: They are revolting. I hate babies.

GEOF: I thought you'd change. Motherhood is supposed to come natural to women.

JO: It comes natural to you, Geoffrey Ingram. You'd make somebody a wonderful wife. What were you talking about to that old mare downstairs?

GEOF: I was giving her the rent. I got my grant yesterday.

JO: You're as thick as thieves, you two.

GEOF: She's going to make the baby a cradle.

JO: What?

GEOF: You know, she makes wicker baskets.

JO: A wicker basket!

GEOF: It's the best we can do, unless you want to go down to the river plaiting reeds.

JO: I don't want her poking her nose into my affairs.

GEOF: You're glad enough to have me dancing attendance on you.

JO: Only because I thought you'd leave me alone. Why don't you leave me alone? [*She cries and flings herself down on the couch.*] I feel like throwing myself in the river.

GEOF: I wouldn't do that. It's full of rubbish.

JO: Well that's all I am, isn't it?

GEOF: Stop pitying yourself.

JO: Don't jump down my throat.

GEOF: How much longer is this going on?

JO: What?

GEOF: Your present performance.

JO: Nobody asked you to stay here. You moved in on me, remember, remember? If you don't like it you can get out, can't you? But you wouldn't do that, would you, Geoffrey? You've no confidence in yourself, have you? You're afraid the girls might laugh . . .

GEOF: Read that book and shut up. When the baby comes, if it ever does, you won't know one end of it from the other.

JO: *Looking After Baby*. Isn't that nice? Three months, exercises, constipation. Four months, relaxation. It even tells you how to wash nappies. How lovely. There's a little job for you, Geoffrey.

GEOF: Drink that. [*He hands her a glass of milk.*]

JO [*flirting with him*]: Does it tell you how to feed babies, Geoffrey?

GEOF: Even you know that.

JO: I know about that way, breast feeding, but I'm not having a little animal nibbling away at me, it's cannibalistic. Like being eaten alive.

GEOF: Stop trying to be inhuman. It doesn't suit you.

JO: I mean it. I hate motherhood.

GEOF: Well, whether you hate it or not you've got it coming to you so you might as well make a good job of it.

JO: I've got toothache.

GEOF: I've got bloody heartache!

JO: I think you'd like everybody to think this baby's yours, wouldn't you, Geoffrey?

GEOF: Not likely.

JO: After all, you don't show much sign of coming fatherhood, do you? You like babies, don't you, Geof?

GEOF: Yes, I do.

JO [*coquettes with him*]: Geoffrey, have you got any of that toothache cure?

[*He moves away.*]

Geoffrey, have you got any of that toothache cure?

GEOF: The only cure for the toothache is a visit to the dentist. Drink your milk.

JO: I hate milk [*She looks out of the window.*] I never thought I'd still be here in the summer. [*She puts her arms round* GEOF *playfully.*] Would you like to be the father of my baby, Geoffrey?

GEOF: Yes, I would.

[JO *stands in the doorway. The children can be heard singing again.*]

What time is it?

JO: Half-past four by the church clock. Why do you stay here, Geof?

GEOF: Someone's got to look after you. You can't look after yourself.

JO: I think there's going to be a storm. Look at that sky. It's nearly black. And you can hear the kids playing, right over there on the croft.

[*A silence in the room: we hear the children singing.*]

GEOF: What would you say if I started something?

JO: Eh!

GEOF: I said what would you say if I started something?

JO: In my condition I'd probably faint.

GEOF: No, I mean after.

JO: I don't want you.

GEOF: Am I repulsive to you?

JO: You're nothing to me. I'm everything to myself.

GEOF: No, you're not. You're going to need me after.

JO: I won't be here after.

GEOF: Do you still think he might come back?

JO: I've forgotten him.

[*She turns towards him, he to her.*]

GEOF: You do need me, Jo, don't you?

JO: Let go of me. You're squeezing my arm.

GEOF: I've never kissed a girl.

JO: That's your fault.

GEOF: Let me kiss you.

JO: Let go of me. Leave me alone.

[*She struggles but he kisses her.*]

GEOF: How was that for first time?

JO: Practise on somebody else.

GEOF: I didn't mean to hurt you.

JO: Look Geof, I like you, I like you very much, but I don't enjoy all this panting and grunting . . .

GEOF: Marry me, Jo.

JO: Don't breathe all over me like that, you sound like a horse. I'm not marrying anybody.

GEOF: I wouldn't ask you to do anything you didn't want to do.

JO: Yes, you would.

GEOF: Jo, I don't mind that you're having somebody else's baby. What you've done, you've done. What I've done, I've done.

JO: I like you, Geof, but I don't want to marry you.

GEOF: Oh, all right. Anyway, I don't suppose I could live up to that black beast of a prince of yours. I bet you didn't struggle when he made love to you.

JO: It might have been better if I had.

GEOF [*he gives her a bar of chocolate*]: Have some chocolate.

JO: Thanks. Do you want some?

GEOF: No.

JO: Go on.

GEOF: I said no.

JO: You like strawberry cream.

GEOF: I don't want any, Jo. I've made my mind up.

JO: Don't be daft, have some chocolate.

GEOF: No . . . [*She gives a piece of chocolate to him just the same.*]

JO: I think it would be best if you left this place, Geof. I don't think it's doing you any good being here with me all the time.

GEOF: I know that, but I couldn't go away now.

JO: You'll have to go some time. We can't stay together like this for ever.

GEOF: I'd sooner be dead than away from you.

JO: You say that as if you mean it.

GEOF: I do mean it.

JO: Why?

GEOF: Before I met you I didn't care one way or the other – I didn't care whether I lived or died. But now . . .

JO: I think I'll go and lie down. [*She goes to bed and lies across it.*]

GEOF: There's no need for me to go, Jo. You said yourself you didn't want anybody else here and I'm only interested in you. We needn't split up need we, Jo?

JO: I don't suppose so.

[*Music. Enter* HELEN.]

HELEN: Jo! Your beloved old lady's arrived. Well, where is she, Romeo?

GEOF: Don't tell her I came for you.

HELEN: What? Don't mumble.

GEOF: I said don't tell her I came for you.

HELEN: All right, all right. This place hasn't changed much, has it? Still the same old miserable hole. Well, where's the lady in question?

GEOF: In there.

HELEN: What, lazing in bed, as usual? Come on, get up; plenty of girls in your condition have to go out to work and take care of a family. Come on, get up.

JO: What blew you in?

HELEN: Let's have a look at you.

JO: Who told you about me?

HELEN: Nobody.

JO: How did you get to know then?

HELEN: Come on, aren't you going to introduce me to your boy friend? Who is he?

JO: My boy friend. Oh, it's all right, we're so decent we're almost dead. I said who told you about me?

HELEN: Does it matter?

JO: I told you to keep out of my affairs, Geoffrey. I'm not having anybody running my life for me. What do you think you're running? A "Back to Mother" movement?

GEOF: Your mother has a right to know.

JO: She's got no rights where I'm concerned.

HELEN: Oh, leave him alone. You're living off him, by all accounts.

JO: Who've you been talking to? That old hag downstairs?

HELEN: I didn't need to talk to her. The whole district knows what's been going on here

JO: And what has been going on?

HELEN: I suppose you think you can hide yourself away in this chicken run, don't you? Well, you can't. Everybody knows.

GEOF: She won't go out anywhere, not even for a walk and a bit of fresh air. That's why I came to you.

HELEN: And what do you think I can do about it? In any case, bearing a child doesn't place one under an obligation to it.

GEOF: I should have thought it did.

HELEN: Well, you've got another think coming. If she won't take care of herself that's her lookout. And don't stand there looking as if it's my fault.

GEOF: It's your grandchild.

HELEN: Oh, shut up, you put years on me. Anyway, I'm having

nothing to do with it. She's more than I can cope with, always has been.

GEOF: That's obvious.

HELEN: And what's your part in this little Victorian melodrama? Nursemaid?

JO: Serves you right for bringing her here, Geof.

HELEN: It's a funny-looking set-up to me.

JO: It's our business.

HELEN: Then don't bring me into it. Where's the loving father? Distinguished by his absence, I suppose.

JO: That's right.

HELEN [to GEOF]: Did she hear any more of him?

JO: No, she didn't.

HELEN: When I'm talking to the organ grinder I don't expect the monkey to answer.

JO: I could get him back tomorrow if I wanted to.

HELEN: Well, that's nice to know. He certainly left you a nice Christmas box. It did happen at Christmas, I suppose? When the cat's away.

GEOF: You've been away a long time.

HELEN: Oh, you shut up. Sling your hook!

JO: Will you keep out of this, Geoffrey?

HELEN: Well, come on, let's have a look at you. [JO *turns away*.] What's up? We're all made the same, aren't we?

JO: Yes we are.

HELEN: Well then. Can you cut the bread on it yet? [JO *turns*.] Yes, you're carrying it a bit high, aren't you? Are you going to the clinic regularly? Is she working?

GEOF: No, I told you, she doesn't like people looking at her.

HELEN: Do you think people have got nothing better to do than look at you?

JO: Leave me alone.

HELEN: She'd be better off working than living off you like a little bloodsucker.

GEOF: She doesn't live off me.

JO: No, we share everything, see! We're communists too.

HELEN: That's his influence I suppose.

JO: Get out of here. I won't go out if I don't want to. It's nothing to do with you. Get back to your fancy man or your husband, or whatever you like to call him.

[HELEN *begins to chase her*.]

Aren't you afraid he'll run off and leave you if you let him out of your sight?

HELEN: I'll give you such a bloody good hiding in a minute, if you're not careful. That's what you've gone short of!

JO: Don't show yourself up for what you are!

HELEN: You couldn't wait, could you? Now look at the mess you've landed yourself in.

JO: I'll get out of it, without your help.

HELEN: You had to throw yourself at the first man you met, didn't you?

JO: Yes, I did, that's right.

HELEN: You're man mad.

JO: I'm like you.

HELEN: You know what they're calling you round here? A silly little whore!

JO: Well, they all know where I get it from too.

HELEN: Let me get hold of her! I'll knock her bloody head round!

JO: You should have been locked up years ago, with my father.

HELEN: Let me get hold of her!

GEOF: Please, Jo, Helen, Jo, please!

HELEN: I should have got rid of you before you were born.

JO: I wish you had done. You did with plenty of others, I know.

HELEN: I'll kill her. I'll knock the living daylights out of her.

GEOF: Helen, stop it, you will kill her!

JO: If you don't get out of here I'll . . . jump out of the window.

[*There is a sudden lull*.]

GEOF [*yelling*]: Will you stop shouting, you two?

HELEN: We enjoy it.

GEOF: Helen!

HELEN: Now you're going to listen to a few home truths, my girl.

JO: We've had enough home truths!

HELEN: All right, you thought you knew it all before, didn't you? But you came a cropper. Now it's "poor little Josephine, the tragedy queen, hasn't life been hard on her". Well, you fell down, you get up . . . nobody else is going to carry you about. Oh, I know you've got this pansified little freak to lean on, but what good will that do you?

JO: Leave Geof out of it!

HELEN: Have you got your breath back? Because there's some more I've got to get off my chest first.

JO: You don't half like the sound of your own voice.

GEOF: If I'd known you were going to bully her like this I'd never have asked you to come here.

HELEN: You can clear off! Take your simpering little face out of it!

JO: Yes, buzz off, Geof! Well, who brought her here? I told you what sort of a woman she was. Go and . . . go and make a cup of tea.

[*He goes.*]

HELEN: Look at your arms. They're like a couple of stalks! You look like a ghost warmed up. And who gave you that haircut, him? Don't sit there sulking.

JO: I thought it was the tea break.

HELEN: I didn't come here to quarrel.

JO: No?

HELEN: I brought you some money.

JO: You know what you can do with that.

HELEN: All right! You've said your piece. Money doesn't

grow on trees. I'll leave it on the table. Have you been collecting your maternity benefit or . . .

JO: Or are you too idle to walk down to the post office? Don't be daft ! I'm not entitled to it. I haven't been earning long enough.

HELEN: You've no need to go short of anything.

JO: It's taken you a long time to come round to this, hasn't it?

HELEN: What?

JO: The famous mother-love act.

HELEN: I haven't been able to sleep for thinking about you since he came round to our house.

JO: And your sleep mustn't be disturbed at any cost.

HELEN: There'll be money in the post for you every week from now on.

JO: Until you forget.

HELEN: I don't forget things; it's just that I can't remember anything. I'm going to see you through this whether you like it or not. After all I am . . .

JO: After all you are my mother! You're a bit late remembering that, aren't you? You walked through that door with that man and didn't give me a second thought.

HELEN: Why didn't you tell me?

JO: You should have known. You're nothing to me.

[PETER *appears.*]

PETER: What the hell's going on? Do you expect me to wait in the filthy street all night?

HELEN: I told you to stay outside.

PETER: Don't point your bloody finger at me.

HELEN: I said I'd only be a few minutes and I've only been a few minutes. Now come on, outside!

PETER: Ah! The erring daughter. There she is. [*Sings.*] "Little Josephine, you're a big girl now." Where d'you keep the whisky?

HELEN: They haven't got any. Now, come on.

PETER [*seeing* GEOF]: What's this, the father? Oh Christ, no!

GEOF: Who's he?

HELEN: President of the local Temperance Society!

PETER [*singing*]: "Who's got a bun in the oven? Who's got a cake in the stove?"

HELEN: Leave her alone.

PETER: Oh, go to hell!

JO: I've got nothing to say . . .

PETER: Go on, have your blasted family reunion, don't mind me! [*Notices* GEOF *again.*] Who's this? Oh, of course! Where are the drinks, Lana? [*He falls into the kitchen, singing.*] "Getting to know you, getting to know all about you . . ."

HELEN: Jo, come on . . .

[*There is a loud crash in the kitchen.*]

And the light of the world shone upon him.

[PETER *enters.*]

PETER: Cheer up, everybody. I am back. Who's the lily? Look at Helen, well, if she doesn't look like a bloody unrestored oil painting. What's the matter everybody? Look at the sour-faced old bitch! Well, are you coming for a few drinks or aren't you?

HELEN: The pubs aren't open yet.

JO: Do you mind getting out of here?

PETER: Shut your mouth, bubble belly! Before I shut it for you. Hey! [*To* GEOF.], Mary, come here. Did I ever tell you about the chappie who married his mother by mistake?

JO: I said get him out of here, Helen. His breath smells.

HELEN: I can't carry him out, can I?

PETER: His name was Oedipus, he was a Greek I think. Well, the old bag turned out to be his mother . . .

HELEN: Shut up, Peter, for God's sake!

PETER: So he scratched out both his eyes

T.H.—E

HELEN: Cut the dirty stories!

PETER: But I only scratched out one of mine. Well, are you coming or not?

HELEN: I'm not.

PETER: Well, is anybody coming for a few drinks? You staying with the ladies, Jezebel?

GEOF: Listen, mister, this is my friend's flat . . .

PETER: And what do you do, Cuddles? Don't worry, I know this district. Look at Helen, isn't she a game old bird? Worn out on the beat but she's still got a few good strokes left.

HELEN: Get out of here, you drunken sot.

PETER: Now I told you to moderate your language. What's this? Giving my money away again?

HELEN: Take your bloody money and get out!

PETER: Thank you.

HELEN: You dirty bastard!

PETER: You should have heard her the other night. You know what happened? Her wandering boy returned. He hadn't been home for two weeks and do you know why? He picked up a couple of grapefruit on a thirty-two bust, rich, young and juicy . . . hey! Where's the smallest room?

GEOF: This way.

PETER: And she went off the deep end. [*Sings as he goes. Another crash offstage.*]

HELEN [*to* GEOF]: You'd better go with him or Lord knows where he'll end up.

GEOF: I hope the landlady hasn't heard him.

HELEN: Cigarette?

JO: No. Yes, I will. I'll keep it for Geof.

HELEN: You'd better have the whole bloody packet if you're in such a state.

JO: Well, he couldn't hold it any more, could he?

HELEN: No one could hold that much.

JO: How long has he been like this?

HELEN: What does that boy friend of yours do for a living?

JO: He's an art student. I suppose that's what's been keeping you occupied?

HELEN: An art student. I might have known. Does he live here?

JO: Why should I answer your questions? You never answer any of mine.

HELEN: Look at you! Why don't you take a bit of pride in yourself? Grow your hair properly?

JO: Look at you. Look what your pride in yourself has done for you.

HELEN: Come and stay with me, Jo; there's a nice room and plenty of food.

JO: No, thanks.

HELEN: You prefer to stay in this hole with that pansified little freak?

GEOF: Shall I go?

HELEN: I didn't know you'd come.

JO: Would you go and live with her if you were me, Geof?

GEOF: No, I don't think I would.

JO: Neither would anybody in their right mind.

GEOF: She always said you were a pretty rotten sort of woman. I thought she was exaggerating.

HELEN: Look, can't you get it into your stupid head that I'm offering you a decent home?

[PETER *enters, more sober, more unpleasant.*]

PETER: Bloody cockroaches are playing leapfrog in there.

HELEN: Look, I'll tell you again, in front of him, my home is yours.

PETER: Ah! Shut up!

HELEN: I'll take care of you and see you through it.

JO: The time to have taken care of me was years ago, when I couldn't take care of myself.

HELEN: All right, but we're talking about here and now. When

T.H.–E*

I really set out to take care of somebody I usually do the job properly.

JO: So I see.

PETER: I'm not having that bloody slut at our place. I'll tell you that for nothing.

HELEN: Take no notice. The house is half mine.

PETER: Like hell it is. I could throw you out tomorrow.

JO: I don't think . . .

PETER: And don't bring that little fruitcake parcel either! [*Mumbles.*] I can't stand the sight of him. Can't stand 'em at any price.

HELEN: Oh, keep out of it. Jo, I can't bear to think of you sitting here in this dump!

PETER: Neither can I. Now let's get going.

HELEN: The whole district's rotten, it's not fit to live in.

PETER: Let's go before we grow old sitting here.

HELEN: Shut up, the pubs will be open in ten minutes.

PETER: You're wrong there. [*Looking at his watch.*] They're open now. What time do you make it?

GEOF: There's one thing about this district, the people in it aren't rotten. Anyway, I think she's happier here with me than in that dazzling white house you're supposed to be so . . .

PETER: Dazzling bunch of bul . . . lot of bloody outsiders, no class at all. What's the time anyway?

HELEN [*to* GEOF]: You shut up! I know what she needs if she's not going to finish up in a box.

PETER: What's the time by your watch, sonny?

GEOF: It's never been right since it last went wrong.

PETER: Neither have I. How long are we going to sit around in this room? I don't like the smell of unwashed bodies, woman. I dragged you out of the gutter once. If you want to go back there it's all the same to me. I'm not having this shower at any price. I'm telling you for the last time because I'm getting out of it. Stay if you want, it's all the same to

me; it's your own bloody level. Well, are you coming or
not?

HELEN: I'm not.

PETER: I said are you coming?

HELEN: And I said I'm not.

PETER: Well, you can just go and take a flying flip out of the
window. [*He goes.*]

HELEN: I'll . . . I'll . . . would you sooner I stayed here
with you?

JO: No, thanks.

PETER: Helen . . . [*Calling.*] . . . come on!

HELEN: I'll send you some money.

JO: Keep it. You might need it.

PETER: Helen!

HELEN: Go to . . .

PETER: Are you coming?

HELEN [*yelling*]: Yes. [*To* GEOF.] See that she goes to the clinic
regularly and be sure she gets enough to eat.

GEOF: She has been doing that.

HELEN: I'll see you around. [*She goes.*]

JO: Well, here endeth the third lesson.

GEOF: At least she left you some money. We can get some . . .

JO: He took it back. I got you a cigarette though, love.

GEOF: Oh, smashing! I was out.

[*Music. They dance together. Fade out.*]

SCENE TWO

GEOFFREY *dances in with a mop and bucket and begins to clean
the place.* JO *dances back and sits on the table reading. She
is wearing a long white housecoat and again, in reality, months
have passed between this and the previous scene. Music out.*

JO: "Ninth month, everything should now be in readiness for the little stranger." Where did you find this book, Geoffrey? It reads like *Little Women*.

GEOF: I got it for fourpence off a book barrow.

JO: You've got terrible tendencies, haven't you?

GEOF: How do you mean?

JO: You like everything to be just that little bit out of date, don't you? Clothes, books, women.

GEOF: You've got no choice, have you? I mean you all start by living in the past. Well look, it's all around you, isn't it?

JO: I wonder if we ever catch up with ourselves?

GEOF: I don't know.

JO: Now you're a real Edwardian, aren't you?

GEOF: What's that?

JO: A proper Ted! And me, I'm contemporary.

GEOF. God help us!

JO: I really am, aren't I? I really do live at the same time as myself, don't I?

GEOF: Do you mind? I've just done all that. Oh come on! Get off!

[*He pushes her with the mop.*]

JO: Hey, hey!

GEOF: Women!

JO: You haven't noticed my home dressmaking.

GEOF: No. I've been trying to ignore it. What is it?

JO: A house-coat.

GEOF: It looks more like a badly tailored shroud.

JO: What the well-dressed expectant mother is wearing this year. I feel wonderful. Aren't I enormous?

GEOF: You're clever, aren't you?

JO: What's in the oven, Geoffrey?

GEOF: You what?

JO: What's cooking?

GEOF: A cake.

JO: Mm, you're wonderful, aren't you?

GEOF: Pretty good.

JO: I know, you make everything work. The stove goes, now we eat. You've reformed me, some of the time at any rate.

[GEOFFREY *shifts the sofa. There is old rubbish and dirt under it.*]

GEOF: Oh, Jo!

JO: I wondered where that had got to.

GEOF: Now you know. It's disgusting, it really is.

JO: Oh Geof, the bulbs I brought with me!

GEOF: Haven't you shifted the sofa since then?

JO: They never grew.

GEOF: No, I'm not surprised.

JO: They're dead. It makes you think, doesn't it?

GEOF: What does?

JO: You know, some people like to take out an insurance policy, don't they?

GEOF: I'm a bit young for you to take out one on me.

JO: No. You know, they like to pray to the Almighty just in case he turns out to exist when they snuff it.

GEOF [*brushing under the sofa*]: Well, I never think about it. You come, you go. It's simple.

JO: It's not, it's chaotic—a bit of love, a bit of lust and there you are. We don't ask for life, we have it thrust upon us.

GEOF: What's frightened you? Have you been reading the newspapers?

JO: No, I never do. Hold my hand, Geof.

GEOF: Do you mind? Halfway through this?

JO: Hold my hand.

[*He does.*]

GEOF: Hey, Jo. Come on, silly thing, it's all right. Come on there.

JO: You've got nice hands, hard. You know I used to try and hold my mother's hands, but she always used to pull them away from me. So silly really. She had so much love for everyone else, but none for me.

GEOF: If you don't watch it, you'll turn out exactly like her.

JO: I'm not like her at all.

GEOF: In some ways you are already, you know.

[*She pushes his hand away.*]

Can I go now?

JO: Yes.

GEOF: Thank you very much! [*He is pushing the couch back into position.*]

JO: "And he took up his bed and walked." You can stay here if you tell me what you do. Do you remember, Geoffrey? I used to think you were such an interesting, immoral character before I knew you. I thought you were like that . . . for one thing.

[GEOFFREY *chases her with the mop all through this speech.*]

You're just like an old woman really. You just unfold your bed, kiss me good night and sing me to sleep. Hey, what's the matter? Don't you like living here with me?

GEOF: It has its lighter moments, but on the whole it's a pretty trying prospect.

JO: Why do you wear black shirts? They make you look like a spiv.

GEOF: They do, Jo, but I can't be too particular. Good clothes cost money.

JO: Well, I weigh in with my share, don't I? That's a nice little job you got me, retouching those bloody photographs. What was it supposed to do, prove I was the artistic type? Of course we can't all be art students, going to our expensive art schools, nursing our little creative genius.

GEOF: Must you shout?

JO: I'm Irish.

GEOF: Never mind, it's not your fault.

JO [*laughing*]: I like you.

GEOF: Do you like me more than you don't like me or don't you like me more than you do?

JO: Now you're being Irish.

GEOF: Fine Irishwoman you are. Where did your ancestors fall, in the Battle of Salford Town Hall?

JO: My mother's father was Irish.

GEOF: You'll find any excuse.

JO: And she had me by an Irishman—the village idiot, from what I can make out.

GEOF: What do you mean?

JO: A frolic in a hay loft one afternoon. You see her husband thought sex was dirty, and only used the bed for sleeping in. So she took to herself an idiot. She said he'd got eyes like me.

GEOF: Are you making it up?

JO: He lived in a twilight land, my daddy. The land of the daft.

GEOF: Did she tell you all this?

JO: Yes.

GEOF: I'm not surprised. It sounds like Ibsen's *Ghosts*. I don't know where Helen gets them from, I don't really.

JO: I had to drag it out of her. She didn't want to tell me.

GEOF: That doesn't mean to say it's the truth. Do people ever tell the truth about themselves?

JO: Why should she want to spin me a yarn like that?

GEOF: She likes to make an effect.

JO: Like me?

GEOF: You said it. You only have to let your hair grow for a week for Helen to think you're a cretin.

JO: What?

GEOF: I said you've only got to let your hair grow for a week for Helen to think you're a cretin. She always looks at me as though I should be put away for treatment, doesn't she?

JO: Yes.

GEOF: I know, you don't have to tell me! Have you been worrying about that all these months?

JO: No.

GEOF: You have.

JO: I haven't.

GEOF: Well, I didn't think you could be so daft. Can you see Helen going out with a real loony!

JO: Well, now you put it like that, no, I can't!

GEOF: No, neither can—I don't know. Anyway, who knows who are the fools and the wise men in this world?

JO: I wouldn't be surprised if all the sane ones weren't in the bin.

GEOF: You're probably right. Anyway everyone knows you're as cracked as an old bedbug.

JO [laughing]: Thanks, Geof. You know, you're a cure.

GEOF: I used to be a patrol leader in the Boy Scouts.

JO: So long as you weren't Scoutmaster! You know, I wish she was here all the same.

GEOF: Why? You'd only quarrel. You know you always say you hate the sight of her.

JO: I do.

GEOF: Well then.

JO: She must know my time has almost come. When do your exams finish?

GEOF: On Thursday.

JO: I wonder which day it'll be? Put your arms round me, Geof. I don't want you to be worried while your exams are on.

GEOF: Then you shouldn't have asked me to put my arms round you, should you?

JO: Ah well, it doesn't matter if you fail. In this country the more you know the less you earn.

GEOF: Yes, you're probably right. I've got something for you. Oh Jo, I'm daft at times.

JO: I know that. I was wondering what it was.

GEOF [from his pack he takes a life-sized doll]: There—isn't it nice? I thought you could practise a few holds on it over the weekend. You've got to be able to establish your superiority over the little devils. I don't know where that goes. There, look, isn't it good?

JO [*seeing the doll*]: The colour's wrong.

GEOF: Jo.

JO: The colour's wrong. [*Suddenly and violently flinging the doll to the ground.*] I'll bash it's brains out. I'll kill it. I don't want his baby, Geof. I don't want to be a mother. I don't want to be a woman.

GEOF: Don't say that, Jo.

JO: I'll kill it when it comes, Geof, I'll kill it.

GEOF: Do you want me to go out and find that chap and bring him back? Is that what you want?

JO: I don't want that. I don't want any man.

GEOF: Well, if you're going to feel like that about it you might as well have it adopted. I thought you'd feel differently as time went on.

JO: I won't.

GEOF: Perhaps you will when you see the baby.

JO: No, I won't.

GEOF: Do you still love him?

JO: I don't know. He was only a dream I had. You know, he could sing and he was so tender. Every Christmas Helen used to go off with some boy friend or other and leave me all on my own in some sordid digs, but last Christmas I had him.

GEOF: Your black prince.

JO: What was his name?

GEOF: Prince Ossini.

JO: No, it was Jimmie!

GEOF: Oh well, the dream's gone, but the baby's real enough.

JO: My mother always used to say you remember the first time all your life, but until this moment I'd forgotten it.

GEOF: Do you remember when I asked you to marry me?

JO: Yes.

GEOF: Do you?

JO: No. What did I say?

GEOF: You just went and lay on the bed.

JO: And you didn't go and follow me, did you?

GEOF: No.

JO: You see, it's not marrying love between us, thank God.

GEOF: You mean you just like having me around till your next prince comes along?

JO: No.

GEOF: Oh well, you need somebody to love you while you're looking for someone to love.

JO: Oh Geof, you'd make a funny father. You are a funny little man. I mean that. You're unique.

GEOF: Am I?

JO: I always want to have you with me because I know you'll never ask anything from me. Where are you going?

[GEOFFREY *goes to the kitchen*.]

GEOF: To see the cake.

[JO *follows him*.]

JO: I'll set the cups and we'll have a celebration, then you'll have to study for your exams. It's a bit daft talking about getting married, isn't it? We're already married. We've been married for a thousand years.

[*They march in together from the kitchen, he with the cake, she with the tea things*.]

GEOF [*putting it down*]: Here, look at that. What are you going to call it?

JO: What, the cake?

GEOF [*laughing*]: No, Jo, the baby.

JO: I think I'll give it to you, Geof. You like babies, don't you? I might call it Number One. It'll always be number one to itself.

[HELEN *enters, loaded with baggage as in Act One, Scene One*.]

HELEN: Anybody at home? Well, I'm back. You see, I couldn't stay away, could I? There's some flowers for you, Jo. The barrows are smothered in them. Oh! How I carried that lot from the bus stop I'll never know. The old place looks a bit more cheerful, doesn't it? I say, there's a nice homely smell. Have you been doing a bit of baking? I'll tell you one thing, it's a lovely day for flitting.

JO: Would you like a cup of tea, Helen?

HELEN: Have you got anything stronger? Oh no, course you haven't! Go on, I'll have a cup with you. Let's have a look at you, love. I arrived just in time, by the look of things, didn't I? How are you, love? Everything straightforward? Been having your regular check-up and doing all them exercises and all the things they go in for nowadays? That's a good girl. Have you got everything packed?

JO: Packed?

HELEN: Yes.

JO: But I'm not going into hospital.

HELEN: You're not having it here, are you?

GEOF: Yes, she didn't want to go away.

HELEN: Oh my God, is he still here? I thought he would be.

GEOF: Do you want a piece of cake, Jo?

JO: Yes, please.

HELEN: You can't have a baby in this dump. Why don't you use a bit of sense for once and go into hospital? They've got everything to hand there. I mean, sometimes the first one can be a bit tricky.

GEOF: There's going to be nothing tricky about it; it's going to be perfectly all right, isn't it, Jo?

HELEN: Who do you think you are, the Flying Doctor?

JO: Look, I've made up my mind I want to have it here. I don't like hospitals.

HELEN: Have you ever been in a hospital?

JO: No.

HELEN: Well, how do you know what it's like? Oo! Give me a cup of tea quick.

GEOF: Oh well, we've got a district nurse coming in.

HELEN: Oh my God, my feet are killing me. How I got that lot from the bus stop I'll never know.

JO: Well what are you lugging all the cases about for?

HELEN: I've come to look after you. It's just as well, by the look of things. [*Whispers to* JO.]

JO: Well, it's going to be a bit crowded, you know. Is your husband coming and all? Is he moving in too?

HELEN: There wouldn't be much room for two of us on that couch, would there?

JO: That's Geoffrey's bed.

GEOF: It's all right, Jo, I don't mind moving out.

JO: For Heaven's sake, you don't have to start wilting away as soon as she barges in.

GEOF: I don't.

HELEN. I could do with a drink.

JO: Start barging around just like a bull in a china shop.

HELEN: I've got some lovely things for the baby, Jo. Where did I put them? Where's that other case, Jo? Oh!

GEOF: Jo, will you sit down. I'll get it.

HELEN: Look, love. I've come here to talk to my daughter. Can you make yourself scarce for a bit?

GEOF: I've got to go, we need some things for the weekend.

JO: You don't have to let her push you around.

GEOF. I don't.

HELEN: Oh I do wish he wouldn't mumble. It does get on my nerves. What's he saying?

GEOF: Where's my pack?

JO: What a couple of old women.

GEOF: Look here, Jo!

JO: Look, just a minute will you. I . . . look I . . . there's nothing . . .

GEOF: How can I stay . . .

HELEN: Come here. How long is he going to stick around here
   Bloody little pansy . . .

JO: Look, if you're going to insult Geof . . .

HELEN: I'm not insulting him.

JO: Yes you are.

HELEN: I'm not. I just don't like his style, that's all.

GEOF: It's all right, Mrs. Smith . . .

HELEN: Look, love, I just want five minutes alone with her.
   Do you mind? Is it too much to ask?

GEOF: Do you want any cotton wool?

HELEN: Good God, does he knit an' all?

JO: You don't have to go.

GEOF: Jo, I've got to go, I'll only be a couple of minutes.

JO: There's plenty of stuff in the kitchen. Now look . . .

   [GEOFFREY *goes*.]

HELEN: You don't mean to tell me he's really gone?

JO: Now that you've been rude to my friend . . .

HELEN: What an arty little freak! I wasn't rude to him. I
   never said a word. I never opened my mouth.

JO: Look, he's the only friend I've got, as a matter of fact.

HELEN: Jo! I thought you could find yourself something more
   like a man.

JO: Why were you so nasty to him?

HELEN: I wasn't nasty to him. Besides, I couldn't talk to you
   in front of him, could I? Hey, wait till you see these things
   for the baby.

JO: You hurt people's feelings and you don't even notice.

HELEN: Jo, I just wanted to get rid of him, that's all. Look at
   those, Jo. Look, isn't that pretty, eh? The baby's going to
   be dressed like a prince, isn't he?

JO: We're all princes in our own little kingdom. You're not
   to insult Geoffrey. Will you leave him alone?

HELEN: Hey, look at this Jo, isn't it pretty? Oh, I love babies—
   aren't they lovely?

JO: Has your husband thrown you out?

HELEN: Oh come off it, Jo. I had to be with you at a time like this, hadn't I? And what about this sailor lad of yours, have you made any attempt to trace him? He's entitled to keep his child, you know.

JO: I wouldn't do that, it's degrading.

HELEN: What do you call this set up?

JO: It's all right. There's no need for you to worry about me. I can work for the baby myself.

HELEN: Who's going to look after it when you're out at work? Have you thought about that?

JO: Yes, I have.

HELEN: Well, you can't do two jobs at once, you know. Who's going to nurse it? Him?

JO: That's my business. I can do anything when I set my mind to it.

HELEN: Very clever, aren't you?

JO: There's no need to be so superior. Look where all your swanking's landed you. What does the little lady want— an engagement ring? And now he's thrown you out, hasn't he, and you have to come crawling back here.

HELEN: Well, it was good while it lasted.

JO: Making a fool of yourself over that throw-back.

HELEN: He threw his money about like a man with no arms.

JO: This is my flat now, Helen.

HELEN: It's all right, love, I've got a bit of money put by.

JO: You're a real fool, aren't you?

HELEN: Oh, Jo, look. I'm back aren't I? Forget it. Don't keep on about it.

JO: Do you know what I think?

HELEN: What?

JO: I think you're still in love with him.

HELEN: In love? Me?

JO: Yes.

HELEN: You must be mad.

JO: What happened?

HELEN: He's gone off with his bit of crumpet. Still, it was good while it lasted. Anyway, I'll shift some of this, Jo.

JO: So we're back where we started. And all those months you stayed away from me because of him! Just like when I was small.

HELEN: I never thought about you! It's a funny thing, I never have done when I've been happy. But these last few weeks I've known I should be with you.

JO: So you stayed away—

HELEN: Yes. I can't stand trouble.

JO: Oh, there's no trouble. I've been performing a perfectly normal, healthy function. We're wonderful! Do you know, for the first time in my life I feel really important. I feel as though I could take care of the whole world. I even feel as though I could take care of you, too!

HELEN: Here, I forgot to tell you, I've ordered a lovely cot for you.

JO: We've got one.

HELEN: It's lovely. It's got pink curtains, you know, and frills. (JO *gets wicker basket from under bed.*]
Oh, I don't like that. What is it?

JO: It's wicker work. Geof got it.

HELEN: It's a bit old-fashioned, isn't it?

JO: We like it.

HELEN: Look love, why don't you go and lie down? You look as though you've got a bit of a headache.

JO: Do you wonder?

HELEN: Well, go and have a rest, there's a good girl. I'm going to tidy this place up for you. I'm going to make it just the way you like it. Go on.

JO: Oh no!

HELEN. Go on, Jo. Go on. It looks more like a laundry basket, doesn't it! Oh! The state of this place! We'll never have it right. Living like pigs in a pigsty—

[GEOFFREY *enters.*]

   Oh, you're back are you? Well, come in if you're coming.
GEOF: Where's Jo?
HELEN: She's in bed. Where do you think she is? She's having
   a little sleep, so don't you dare wake her up.
GEOF: I wouldn't do that. [*He places pack filled with food on
   the table.*]
HELEN: Don't put that bag on there, I'm cleaning this place
   up.
GEOF: You know I just did it before you came.
HELEN: It doesn't look like it. Look, son, we're going to have
   the midwife running in and out of here before long. We
   want this place all clean and tidy, all hygienic-looking, if
   that's possible.
GEOF: Well, it's clean.
JO: Is that Geof?
HELEN: Now look what you've done!
GEOF: Yes, Jo.
JO: Have you got any of those headache pills, love?
GEOF: Yes, I'll get you some.
HELEN: If you're going in there take these flowers with you
   and put them in water. You might as well make yourself
   useful. They look as though they're withering away. [*She
   peers into the pack.*] What the devil's he got here? What's
   that? Spaghetti! I don't know how people can eat it. And
   that's a funny looking lettuce. What the hell's that? Hey,
   what's this here?
GEOF: What?
HELEN: All this muck in here?
GEOF: Well, Jo likes that type of food.
HELEN: Since when? She needs proper food down her at a
   time like this.
GEOF: Oh!

   [HELEN *points to wicker basket.*]

HELEN: Hey, you can throw that bloody thing out for a start.

GEOF: What thing?

HELEN: That thing there. You're not putting my grandchild in a thing like that. Oh, this place! It's filthy! I don't know what you've been doing between the two of you. You might have kept it a bit cleaner than this. Just look at it! Don't stand there looking silly holding that thing, throw it away, or do something with it! I've ordered a proper cot of the latest design, it's got all the etceteras and everything. This place! You're living like pigs in a pigsty. Oh, for God's sake give it here, I'll do something with it.

GEOF: Yes, but Jo likes it.

HELEN: Well, I suppose it will come in handy for something. [*She enters the kitchen.*] Oh my God, it's the same in here! Nowhere to put anything . . . Are you off now?

GEOF: Yes.

HELEN: Well, take that muck with you as you,re going.

GEOF: I don't want it.

HELEN: I'm sure I don't.

GEOF: Mrs. Smith, I . . . I . . .

HELEN: Are you talking to me?

GEOF: Yes, I wanted to ask you something.

HELEN: Well, get it said. Don't mumble.

GEOF: I don't want you to take offence.

HELEN: Do I look the type that takes offence?

GEOF: Would you not frighten Jo?

HELEN: I thought you said you were going.

GEOF: I said would you not frighten Jo.

HELEN: What are you talking about, frightening her?

GEOF: You know, telling her that it might be tricky or that she might have trouble, because she's going to be all right.

HELEN: Are you trying to tell me what to do with my own daughter?

GEOF: Oh no.

HELEN: Well, are you going?

GEOF: Yes, although she said she didn't want a woman with her when she had it.

HELEN: She said what?

GEOF: She said she wanted me with her when she had it because she said she wouldn't be frightened if I was with her.

HELEN: How disgusting!

GEOF: There's nothing disgusting about it.

HELEN: A man in the room at a time like this!

GEOF: Husbands stay with their wives.

HELEN: Are you her husband?

GEOF: No.

HELEN: Well, get.

GEOF: I'm going. She can't cope with the two of us. Only just don't frighten her, that's all.

HELEN: I've told you we don't want that.

GEOF: Yes I know, but she likes it.

HELEN: You can bloody well take it with you, we don't want it.

[GEOFFREY *empties food from his pack on to the table while* HELEN *thrusts it back.* HELEN *finally throws the whole thing, pack and all, on to the floor.*]

GEOF: Yes, the one thing civilisation couldn't do anything about—women. Good-bye Jo, and good luck. [*He goes.*]

[JO *stirs on the bed.*]

HELEN: It's all right, love, I'm here and everything's all right. Are you awake now?

JO: Hello. Yes . . . What's it like?

HELEN: What?

JO: Is there much pain?

HELEN: No! It's not so much pain as hard work, love. I was putting my Christmas pudding up on a shelf when you started on me. There I was standing on a chair singing away merry as the day is long . . .

JO: Did you yell?

HELEN: No, I ran.

JO: Do you know, I had such a funny dream just now.

HELEN: Oh Jo, you're always dreaming, aren't you. Well
don't let's talk about your dreams or we'll get morbid.

JO: Where would you like those flowers putting?

HELEN: Over . . . over there . . . Come on, you come and
do it, love.

JO: Hasn't Geof come back yet?

HELEN: No, he hasn't.

JO: Well, where are you going to sleep, Helen?

HELEN: It's all right, love. Don't fall over, now.

JO: You know, I've got so used to old Geof lying there on that
couch like—like an old watchdog. You aren't . . .

HELEN: It's all right, love, don't you worry about me, I'll find
somewhere.

JO: I wonder where he is . . . Oh!

HELEN: Oh Jo, careful . . . Hold on, love, hold on! It'll be
all right. The first one doesn't last long. Oh my God, I
could do with a drink now. Hold on.

[JO *kneels on bed.* HELEN *strokes her hair.*]

JO: That's better.

HELEN: Are you all right now? There we are. [*Children sing
outside.*] Can you hear those children singing over there on
the croft, Jo?

JO: Yes, you can always hear them on still days.

HELEN: You know when I was young we used to play all day
long at this time of the year; in the summer we had singing
games and in the spring we played with tops and hoops,
and then in the autumn there was the Fifth of November,
then we used to have bonfires in the street, and gingerbread
and all that. Have I ever told you about the time when we
went to a place called Shining Clough? Oh, I must have
done. I used to climb up there every day and sit on the top

of the hill, and you could see the mills in the distance, but the clough itself was covered in moss. Isn't it funny how you remember these things? Do you know, I'd sit there all day long and nobody ever knew where I was. Shall I go and make us a cup of tea?

[HELEN *enters kitchen and fiddles with stove.*]

Oh Jo, I've forgotten how we used to light this thing.
JO: Turn on all the knobs. Mind you don't gas yourself.
HELEN: I still can't do it.
JO: Geof'll fix it.
HELEN: No, it's all right.
JO: Helen.
HELEN: Yes.
JO: My baby may be black.
HELEN: You what, love?
JO: My baby will be black.
HELEN: Oh, don't be silly, Jo. You'll be giving yourself nightmares.
JO: But it's true. He was black.
HELEN: Who?
JO: Jimmie.
HELEN: You mean to say that . . . that sailor was a black man? . . . Oh my God! Nothing else can happen to me now. Can you see me wheeling a pram with a . . . Oh my God, I'll have to have a drink.
JO: What are you going to do?
HELEN: I don't know. Drown it. Who knows about it?
JO: Geoffrey.
HELEN: And what about the nurse? She's going to get a bit of a shock, isn't she?
JO: Well, she's black too.
HELEN: Good, perhaps she'll adopt it. Dear God in heaven!
JO: If you don't like it you can get out. I didn't ask you to come here.

HELEN: Where's my hat?

JO: On your head.

HELEN: Oh yes . . . I don't know what's to be done with you, I don't really. [*To the audience.*] I ask you, what would you do?

JO: Are you going?

HELEN: Yes.

JO: Are you just going for a drink?

HELEN: Yes.

JO: Are you coming back?

HELEN: Yes.

JO: Well, what are you going to do?

HELEN: Put it on the stage and call it Blackbird. [*She rushes out.*]

[JO *watches her go, leaning against the doorpost. Then she looks round the room, smiling a little to herself—she remembers* GEOF.]

JO: As I was going up Pippin Hill,
Pippin Hill was dirty.
And there I met a pretty miss,
And she dropped me a curtsy.
Little miss, pretty miss,
Blessings light upon you.
If I had half a crown a day,
I'd gladly spend it on you.

Curtain.